BREAKTHROUGH COURAGE

9 Habits to Conquer Fear

and

Build a Brave Heart

A Manual to Wholehearted Living

Steve Holt, D.D., M.A.

PARLIAMENT.
PRESS

PARLIAMENT.
PRESS

Colorado Springs, CO 80920
Copyright © 2024 by Steve Holt
Printed in the United States of America

Unless otherwise marked, all Scripture quotations are taken from the New King James Version.® Copyright © 1982 by Thomas Nelson. Used by permission. All rights reserved.

Scripture quotations marked **MSG** are taken from *The Message*, copyright © 1993, 2002, 2018 by Eugene H. Peterson. Used by permission of NavPress. All rights reserved. Represented by Tyndale House Publishers.

Scripture quotations marked **NLT** are taken from the *Holy Bible*, New Living Translation, copyright ©1996, 2004, 2015 by Tyndale House Foundation. Used by permission of Tyndale House Publishers, Carol Stream, Illinois 60188. All rights reserved.

ISBN: 9798303055629

Cover Lion Face Illustration by Adam Sullivan
Author Photography by Joshua Holt
Cover Layout by Anna Henderson
'Book Ready' Crafting & Design by AreYouLost Press

Contents

Endorsements

The last five years have brought worldwide turbulence producing fear, anxiety, and depression. Uncertainty about the future is palpable. The times we live in call for faithful, courageous believers who can confidently live out their faith despite the demonic resistance in the broader culture. Such courage is desperately needed but rare, especially in the church. In his new and timely book, Breakthrough Courage, Dr. Steve Holt gives the reader a step-by-step strategy to develop Godly habits which produce the courage required to live abundantly in this challenging period of history. With honesty and vulnerability Steve weaves together biblical truth and personal experience to communicate with us. From the introduction (don't skip the introduction!) through the final chapter Steve outlines steps we can take to become the fully integrated and courageous man or woman God created us to be. This book is a must-read!

> Steven H. Spillers, MD, MA
> Neurologist and Clinical Neurophysiologist

Habits can make or break a person. Pastor Steve Holt's book addresses how to build productive and Godly habits that will make our lives flourish. Pastor Steve speaks from a wealth of experience so we can rely on his words. I know Pastor Steve and am one who trusts him greatly. Readers would do well to do the same.

> Doug Lamborn
> U.S. Congressman

Steve Holt is a faithful pastor and a spiritual entrepreneur who is making a powerful impact for the Kingdom of God. In Breakthrough Courage Steve shares the habits that have shaped him and can transform the lives of those who embrace them. Each chapter teaches, convicts, convinces, inspires, and provides tools for living out the habits. I highly recommend this excellent book!

> Dr. Todd Hudnall
> Senior Pastor of Radiant Church in Colorado Springs

Dr. Steve Holt's latest book, Breakthrough Courage, is a must-read for anyone looking to step out in faith – with the confidence of Christ - and be the person your family, your friends, your workplace and the world needs you to be. No matter your upbringing, education, social status or title, God has created you to do something extraordinary. Dr. Holt takes the reader chapter-by-chapter with encouragement, scriptural references and examples of courageous women and men who embraced tough times and became overcomers. His reminder that we all need "bloodstained allies" particularly touched my heart and took me back to the moment I unexpectedly became a widow, at age 44, and was suddenly a single mom to a teenager we had adopted out of the foster care system just a year prior. It was my friends, my sisters-in-Christ, who walked with me, cried with me, reminded me that they'd walk with me every step of the way. It was this period of trauma and grief in my life that was shaping me for what God had planned since he formed me in the womb: the result of a one-night-stand and almost aborted at a clinic in Mexico, but then adopted after my birth mother chose life. I experienced the Breakthrough Courage that we all need to fulfill our calling. I am getting this book for everyone on our staff!"

> Diane Ferraro
> CEO, Save the Storks

I believe we are living in a new world since the pandemic. Plagued by fear, anxiety, depression, along with all the mental struggles social media can bring into life. These last 4 years have exponentially increased the challenges in people's lives and it's more important now than ever to have Breakthrough Courage. In a world where we are severally lacking it, Dr. Steve Holt lays out the road to get back to having courage. So, take heart, go on this journey, and start to develop good habits for your life in order to have Breakthrough Courage!

Charlie Woerner
2023 Super Bowl, Tight End Atlanta Falcons

All I can say is WOW! This book does a great job of not only addressing the things that most pastors try to avoid but it's done in such a practical and informative way. Breakthrough Courage hits on all of the strategic cornerstones used by the "great deceiver" to steal our identity, kill our hope and destroy our testimony. This book and the practical steps of life application is a game changer and has the potential to be the catalyst that empowers people to step up, quit making excuses, and become overcomers.

Jim Garrett
Serial Entrepreneur, Investor, and Board Member in Business and Ministry

"This book is biblical, personal and practical. You can go through it yourself or with others. I love the stories and research that back up biblical truth. The questions at the end of each chapter bring it home. It will change your life for the good...if you put the habits into practice."

Pastor David Holt
Living Hope Church; Athens, Georgia

In a world filled with fear, anxiety, and depression, Breakthrough Courage provides a pathway to stay grounded, keep your sanity, and grow in life. Pastor Steve's guidance takes courage to follow, but even adopting two of his eight lessons can strengthen your faith and transform you. Pastor Steve shares incredibly transparent and authentic stories about his life, offering lessons we can all learn from and apply to our own lives. His honesty and vulnerability makes Breakthrough Courage deeply impactful and relatable.

Amy Stephens
Former Colorado State House Majority Leader

I believe we are on the threshold of the most spectacular days in human history! The Lord of Hosts is looking for a Company of "everyday" believers to rise up with faith-fueled courage and lead the way into our promised tomorrows! Steve not only proposes that this Breakthrough Courage is attainable, but lays out a practical pathway to get there...the very steps which have been proven out in his own journey. We CAN break through the "spectator / hero" divide and enter into our own Promised Land of Wholehearted living! I challenge you to not just read, but DO this book. Better yet, why not gather a few "bloodstained allies" and work through it together?!"

Jim Mafuccio
Managing Director, Aspen Funds, Host of KingSpeak Podcast

In Breakthrough Courage, Steve Holt has once again demonstrated a unique ability to connect with us and challenge us. He does so on Page 1 and on every single subsequent page of this fantastic new book. Steve keeps it simple; he shares the truth and helps us understand the obvious and then he shows us how to take the necessary steps toward real meaningful change. He is authentic and winsome and confidently vulnerable. He knows that he can be this way with us because of his own strong and deep relationship with Christ. This book can change your life. I hope you have the courage to read it!

    Christopher Gould
    SVP/GM National Programming & Ministry Relations, Salem Media Group

I believe wholeheartedly that Breakthrough Courage comes only from a place of total completeness in Christ. From this place, we are equipped and empowered to GIVE courageously, rather than striving out of emptiness to 'get.' Dr. Steve Holt, my Pastor for over 14 years, has consistently led by example in this area. In our lives, we become what we repeatedly do. If we lead ourselves and others into Breakthrough Courage from total fullness in Christ like Steve has done for me, the world can change! My prayer is that you will not only read this book but also examine yourself and apply its principles. We need leaders like Steve, and we need leaders like you. Step boldly into Breakthrough Courage today!

    Matthew Doyon
    "Zealous" on YouTube, 4,000,000+ Zealots and Counting

Acknowledgments

This book came out of the furnace of relationships. If you read the entire book, you may notice that all my examples come from real-life situations that have brought deep pain and great joy. It's in connection with people that I have observed the value of good and bad habits. I have seen some of the most talented yet fearful people squander their lives through the inability to harness their time. But I've also watched very normal, even below-average folks skyrocket in courage and tenacity through harnessing their time effectively.

I want to thank those who have sacrificed their time and talents to help me make this book a reality. They are the ones who actually live out the contents of this book.

- My wife, Liz, for her constant support, critiques, and love. She likes to say she's the "military aid" in my leadership. That she is! When I was struggling to find the right words, she peppered me with her grammar tips. (She was an English major at UCLA, what can I say?) She also came up with the title!

- My executive pastor, Ryan Styre, for always being the first guy at my side in all things and for coming up with the subtitle for this book!

- Jay Inman for formatting the pages of this book. He's always fired up to help me in anything.

- Adam Sullivan, for his incredible lion face illustration on the book cover.

- Anna Henderson, my beautiful and creative first-born daughter, for her cover layout. She worked on the cover while rocking an infant. That's what I call multitalented and multitasking!

- Karla Dial, the best editor in the world! We did it Karla, our third book together. You're amazing!

- Chandler Holt, my daughter-in-law for her expert advice and content in Habit 8. I'm a lot healthier because of your tips.
- Pamela Holloway, for her advice and additions to Habit 8. You were a key part of our church soldiering through COVID.
- The elders at The Road Church who allowed me a "study break" to write this book. High fives to Ryan Styre, Scott Heyler, Josh Personius, Case Boogaard, Sherm Moats, Richard Dutt, Leon Goeas, Steve Clark, and Doug Guilzon.
- To my dad, Pastor Joe Holt, who is now ninety-two years old and has lived out the contents of this book. He was my first model of how to live a productive, relational, and successful life.
- Samuel Holt, my attorney son, who did the first edits and made huge suggestions in how to organize my thoughts better.
- Pierre and Pam Doyon, Nelly and Brett Mayer for your friendship, prayers, and first round of editing.
- Jan Inman and Judy Dutt (The Comma Hammer) for your final edit.
- I have so appreciated some of my cigar brothers who read and sent me ideas for the book: Kyle Barber, Mike McNeil, Dirk Hobbs, and Chris Gould.
- The pastors and staff at The Road Church for giving me their thoughts on the title for the book.
- The Bloodstained Allies of my life, who have lived out the convictions of this book around my fire pit for many years: Ryan Styre, Jay Inman, Andy Popovich, Mark McWilliams, Josh Personius, Al McClausland, Brian Michaels, Jeff Anderson, David Holt, Jeff Paulk, and Jim Garrett. Also, thanks for the great cigars and the ideas for the book.
- My family, who has given me the motivation to stay in the fight even during some dark times (covered in Habits 3 and

4): Liz, Dad, David & Dede, Anna & Joe, Daniel & Chandler, Ethan & Deborah, Isaac and Ana, Samuel, Josh & Mary, and Charity. They've seen it all.

- For the four hundred-plus "Wholehearted Men" who fill our sanctuary every Tuesday morning at 6 a.m. to listen to me, have a hearty breakfast, and then share their hearts with each other as bloodstained allies. Much of this book came from the formation of my messages for Tuesday mornings.

- The battle-tested, faithful, and energetic members of The Road Church. All of you have been in the fight of building a great church. We have worked out these convictions together in real time.

*"Quality is not an act,
it is a habit."*

Aristotle

Fear is a reaction.

Courage is a decision.

Winston Churchill

The quality of our lives often depends on the quality of our habits.

With the same habits, you'll end up with the same results.

But with better habits, anything is possible.

James Clear

Introduction:
Habits Define You

He grew up a slave. All he had ever known was a culture plagued with fear and intimidation. On his back he carried the scars of bondage. He recalled the stories from his parents—stories of a past marked by freedom. But that had all happened before he was born. From earliest childhood, his was a life of taskmasters ruling over his every move.

Finally, he stood at the river of freedom, clutching the remnants of hope for new promises, new beginnings. But after forty years of wandering in the wastelands, that hope was unrealized and nearly gone. He could feel the familiar feelings of fear and anxiety rising. Even with the cloud of God's presence around him, mentoring from his spiritual father, and the victories in battle he had experienced many times, fear had again gripped him. But despite his fear, Joshua was being called to lead his people—to actualize God's promise for Israel.

Moses, who had emancipated the Israelites from Egyptian slavery, had guided and instructed Joshua over the last forty years in the wilderness. Under his tutelage, Joshua had already led the army of Israel to victory over the Amalekites (Exodus 17:13), climbed Mt. Sinai (Exodus 24:13–18), and spied out the Promised Land (Numbers 13–14) and saw that it was good.

A New Kind of Courage

Moses knew Joshua well and understood he was ready for the challenges of leadership. But Moses, sensing his fear and trepidation, took him up a mountain and told him forthrightly and boldly three times: "Be strong and courageous" (Deuteronomy 31:6–7, 23).

Trembling under the weight of his growing responsibilities, Joshua was still unsure of himself. The memories of old bondages and

3

failures still coursed through his thinking. Joshua needed a new kind of courage—breakthrough courage—if he was going to fulfill God's destiny for his life. So God directly spoke to him four times more: "Be strong and courageous!" (Joshua 1:6–7, 9, and 18).

God doesn't repeat a command unless it's necessary. Joshua needed to shed his slavish, fearful mentality—and to do so, he needed to hear those words again: "Have I not commanded you? Be strong and of good courage; do not be afraid" (Joshua 1:9). In fact, between the admonitions of Moses and the commands of God, Joshua heard *seven times*, "Be strong and courageous!"

> *Despite his fears, Joshua did become strong and courageous! With breakthrough courage, the former slave of Egypt became the leader of Israel. Joshua learned to conquer his fears, and in doing so became one of the bravest men in the Bible. God can do the same thing in your life!*

Joshua's courageous leadership would truly inaugurate breakthrough—not just in his personal life, but in the life of his nation. His breakthrough courage eventually led to the Israelites conquering Canaan, dividing the Promised Land, and establishing the kingdom of Israel. Joshua learned to overcome fear, doubt, and depressing circumstances. He courageously stepped into his calling and purpose—not with a lack of fear, but despite it.

You also need a new kind of courage—breakthrough courage. Author and University of Houston research professor Brené Brown has said that "fear is that limbic drive to armor up and self-protect."[1] Breakthrough courage means identifying your deepest fears and working through them. It means crossing into the Promised Land of your life despite the fear standing in your way. You may be standing at a river of fear, a barrier to your calling. But God has promised you a destiny on the other side of your river of doubt.

Our world is a frightening place, and very few people currently are walking out their destiny and calling because they are shackled down by fear.

Introduction

Fearful Times

A 2023 Gallup Poll titled "World Unhappier, More Stressed than Ever" concluded that:

> The [COVID] pandemic is not entirely to blame for the increase in negative emotions. Gallup's data show that the world has been on a negative trajectory for a decade.[2]

Likewise, a national poll of eighteen- to twenty-nine-year-olds conducted by Harvard's Institute of Politics revealed that nearly two-thirds (64 percent) of young Americans have "more fear than hope about the future."[3]

Another poll conducted in late 2022 by the American Psychiatric Association revealed that about two out of every five Americans rated their mental health as fair or poor. The following three areas were ranked as the highest causes of anxiety:

> 70 percent are worried about the safety of their families; 68 percent are anxious about the safety of their identity; and 66 percent are fearful [about]their health.[4]

Recently, I met with the assistant to the mayor of my city, and asked, "What do you believe to be the number one problem in our city?" He answered, "Mental health and fear."

We are living in one of the most fearful times in the history of our nation, and it's taking a toll on our mental health. Like Joshua, we need to hear God tell us, "Be strong and courageous."

Breakthrough Courage

So how is *your* anxiety level? Like Joshua, do you experience overwhelming fear that hinders you from overcoming the challenges set before you? Do you need a breakthrough of courage in your life?

The phrase "fear not" appears 144 times in the Bible, and "courage" is mentioned 114 times! Fear and courage are major biblical themes. In fact, I propose that fear and courage are not mutually exclusive but intricately intertwined.

Winston Churchill, who was prime minister of Great Britain during World War II and arguably the greatest leader in England's long history, once said, "Fear is a reaction. Courage is a decision."[5] We all want to avoid the hard things, the scary things in life—that is natural to being human. Courage requires us to make a conscious choice in the storm of apprehension.

Courage is not the absence of distress but rather consistently deciding to act despite your anxiety until a breakthrough comes. This book will show you how to develop new habits that will empower you to master your fears and live from a whole heart.

Learning to be strong and courageous in the valley of fear is one of the lessons of life that few master. But it is a lesson essential to living a fulfilling, meaningful life, and the key to wholehearted living. Each day requires one to use a certain amount of courage. Just think about it: We need courage to navigate difficult relationships. We need courage to get married. We need courage to become a loving, effective parent. We need courage to stand up again when we've fallen in defeat.

Living an effective and successful life is not for cowards. It's for those who recognize their fears and still choose bravery.

We have been created in the image of God, and that means the Lord has designed all of us with the ability to experience breakthrough courage. Such courage is not the product of personality or good fortune. It is the result of our everyday thoughts, decisions, and actions that become habits.

Habits Harness Time

A habit is an action or routine that is performed regularly until it becomes automatic. Our days largely consist of our habits. Most of us probably have a daily ritual we diligently follow. We drink our morning coffee, take our kids to school, go to work, go to the gym, make the same dinner we did last week, and maybe stare into the freezer for a while, trying to decide whether to eat the ice cream or not, before we go to bed. Researchers at Duke University found that 40 percent of our daily actions reflect learned habits.[6] In his book *The Common Rule: Habits of Purpose for an Age of Distraction*, Justin Early writes, "We are all living according to a specific regimen of habits, and those habits shape most of our life."[7]

Habits harness time and energy; time is the currency of purpose. This means that our purpose and destiny are largely determined by the habits we develop.

Habits make us more efficient. Doing something repeatedly in the same way means that we don't have to think about all the intricate details of our actions. For instance, when he's not being called to account before Congress, Mark Zuckerberg, the founder of Facebook, wears the same style of T-shirt and pants to work every day because he says it saves him time worrying about what to wear. We know how to do something because we've already done it before—many times. Have you ever pulled into your driveway and then realized you didn't even remember the drive home? That's the power of a habit.

Our use of time determines the quality of our lives. James Clear, author of the *New York Times* bestselling book *Atomic Habits,* writes,

> The quality of our lives often depends on the quality of our habits. With the same habits, you'll end up with the same results. But with better habits, anything is possible.[8]

We become what we repeatedly do; our lives will never improve until we transform our daily habits. It is in this restructuring of our habits that we transform our character as well. The legendary football coach Vince Lombardi once said,

"Watch your actions, they become your habits. Watch
your habits, they become your character."9

We will never change our lives unless we change something we do
daily. Habits have little to do with feelings, inspiration, or enthusiasm.
Habits are actions repeatedly done based on our purpose. Actions
build habits; habits determine our character; and character determines
our future.

Developing the right habits in our lives has compounding effects.
Think about the economic principle of compounding interest. At
first, interest accrues only on the principal of our investment. But
quickly, it begins accruing on the interest that has accumulated as
well—and suddenly, the investment reaps exponential benefits far
beyond the initial amount. After graduation from college, I invested
seven thousand dollars in four companies on the stock market. I
never touched the money. When I decided to go to graduate school
ten years later, my initial investment had grown to over one hundred
thousand dollars!

It is the same with habits. Habits accrue interest, and accumulated
habits, over time, bring breakthrough. As you will discover in this
book, I will share nine habits that each have a compounding effect in
your life that, when used together, will bring exponential increase.
Each habit builds on the others.

*These nine habits will be deposits in the bank of courage that incrementally
empower you to master fears in your life and build a brave heart. Each
habit is another investment with the compound interest of changing your life!*

Do a Little a Lot

Successfully changing your life isn't as hard as you may think. Too
often we think it will only come from monumental shifts—that slight
changes have little or no effect. It's easy to think that, considering we
are inundated with news stories of nobodies achieving stardom or
winning the lottery overnight. Though these stories are usually

inspiring, they trick us into thinking that cosmic changes in our life are all it takes to lead to transformation. But don't be deceived: Research shows that it's the small, incremental habits over a long period of time that make the greatest difference.

> The difference a tiny improvement can make over time is astounding. Here's how the math works out: if you can get 1 percent better each day for one year, you'll end up thirty-seven times better by the time you're done.[10]

A little, done often, makes a big difference. Small habit changes over time can bring massive breakthrough. I learned this while serving as a missionary in Japan.

A little background: I was never good at learning languages in high school. The only way I passed my Spanish class was because my gymnastics coach was my Spanish teacher, and he needed me to pass his class in order to be eligible to compete. So, as a missionary, knowing my lack of skill in language acquisition, I had to create a new strategy.

I came up with a simple two-step plan. First, each day I would walk onto a college campus in Tokyo and strike up a conversation in Japanese for a minimum of ten minutes. No English, only Japanese. Thankfully, it was easy to find Japanese students willing to speak in their native tongue to an American eager to learn their language. And it was fun to build friendships at the same time. Those ten-minute conversations didn't amount to much at first, but I could see incremental language breakthroughs every week.

The second new habit involved learning one to two new Japanese sentence structures per week. It was gradual and methodical, but over a two-year span, it was highly effective. Breakthrough came, and eventually I was giving speeches and sermons in Japanese. Incremental but consistent habits have compounding effects over time.

Breakthrough Courage

From Habits to Identity

A change in the way we perceive our identity is the key to transformation. Our actions will reform how we see ourselves, which in turn will revolutionize our lives! If we don't experience a shift in our identity with a new habit, rarely will the habit last.

> *My cultural identity had to become a part of my conversation. In a sense, I had to start thinking in Japanese, not in English. I was being inwardly changed through my new habit.*

To return to my study of Japanese: As I studied the language through conversations with students, I noticed a change in my identity. Even the sentence structure of the language impacted my understanding of myself. In English, most sentences proceed in the following order: subject, verb, and then direct object—but the grammatical structure of Japanese is subject, object, and verb. However, in Japanese, the subject is sometimes, but not always, left out. For example, we would say in English, "I want to eat." But in Japanese you might say "want eat," which in English would be both an incomplete sentence and an awkward thing to say.

I had to learn when and where to leave off the subject. How did I determine that? It wasn't easy. It was less about grammar and more intuitive and cultural. I had to feel out a discussion and understand the context of the conversation. I needed to enter the other speaker's world and connect to the meaning of our dialogue. I had to shift from thinking like an American to thinking like a Japanese person.

The initial motivation to start a new habit often begins with some extrinsic motivation, like "I want to lose twenty-five pounds so I will look better." But if the extrinsic habit isn't changed into intrinsic motivation, it likely will not last. To *want* something is a great starting point, but unless you *become* something, you will rarely continue. Until the habit becomes who you *are*, it will be short-lived.

But none of this is possible if we don't have the courage to develop new habits.

Introduction

Wholehearted Courage

It takes courage to desire change in our lives. The root of the word "courage" is *cor*, the Latin word for "heart." It's the root word in "cardiologist"—meaning a heart doctor. When I use the word "wholehearted" in this book, I am talking about the courage it takes to be honest about who you are, to tell your story with your whole heart—the breakthrough courage it takes to move past your fear to be authentic about unmentionable things like shame and failure. Breakthrough courage is only found in wholly owning your story and allowing God's Spirit to change you. These nine habits will challenge you to discover your true heart, your true identity, and to wholeheartedly live with authenticity and bravery.

The word "courage" also means "to speak out or declare." According to clinical psychologist and bestselling author Carla Marie Manly, when we express our thoughts out loud, we become more aware of what is going in our mind. Studies show speaking convictions out loud creates new proteins in our brain. Saying things out loud means we access the brain's language center and become more intentional about our thoughts and actions.[11]

When we declare our identity out loud, we are expressing wholehearted courage! Being willing to live authentically is difficult and scary. Being authentic means we must be honest about our shortcomings, our mistakes, our pain, and our messed-up past. But we can only improve ourselves and develop better habits if we are honest about what needs to change.

What Is Your Trajectory?

Growing into a courageous person will not happen overnight. It doesn't matter how successful or unsuccessful you are right now. Your current state is not the issue. *Don't stress over your current condition.* The real questions is: Are you on a *trajectory* that will eventually lead to success? You should be much more concerned about the trajectory of your new habits than your current success or lack thereof.

Wholeheartedly committing to small, incremental healthy habit changes will shift the trajectory of your life. We tend to overfocus on our current state but underfocus on the direction we are headed. This book will challenge you to stay the course through simple, cumulative, and focused habits that will, over time, change your destiny.

The wholehearted person is one who is honest about their fears, shortcomings, and mistakes, but is bravely determined to get better through incremental changes in life. They have surrendered their daily life to good habits. Their identity is being transformed by their willingness to face their fears and take on brave new habits.

In this book I will introduce nine habits that I believe can be the catalyst to breakthrough changes in your life. These habits are based in spiritual, psychological, and scientific research, as well as the anecdotes of leaders and other people who have lived courageous and brave lives.

I have seen the power of habits change my own life. From the changes I needed to make as a husband and father, a pastor and entrepreneur—and as you'll learn in this book, the habits that came out of my own brokenness and mistakes—I have discovered that courage can bring breakthrough. Anyone can change their life through changing their habits. I've seen normal people *become* powerful leaders through disciplined changes in their daily routine. I believe that these nine habits will bring new joy, new relationships, and a new direction in your life.

Micro-Progressions

Building new habits is anything but easy. If it were, everyone would be doing it. But healthy habits can and will transform *you*. Small progressions over time will compound into a new life.

These nine habits, continually and incrementally done, can transform your life from the armor of fear to the freedom of courage. Those changes I promise are hard at first, but the result is a better you and a better life.

Introduction

The nine habits are reinforced at the end of each chapter with a few exercises: an identity declaration to say *out loud,* and discussion questions for you to ponder and journal about. My prayer is that through this book, you will become like Joshua, who with breakthrough courage discovered his destiny. My hope is that the fears that have plagued your heart and mind will gradually be conquered through your new habits. Let's get to work—together!

Dr. Steve Holt
Colorado Springs, Colorado

Seeking first the Kingdom of God…is the most
profound and noble statement ever made to
man.

Dr. Jordan Peterson

"Therefore, do not worry…
For your heavenly Father knows that you need
all these things. But seek first the
Kingdom of God
and His righteousness,
and all these things shall be added to you.

Jesus
Matthew 6:30–33

Habit 1
Seek the First Thing First

P eople are fearful—and social media and the twenty-four-hour news cycle aren't making things better. From pharmaceutical ads to quick-fix infomercials, the media traffics in fear. It sells, and we're buying.

Depression is at an all-time high, and still skyrocketing. In 2023, the National Institute of Health found that more than twenty-one million Americans struggle with some form of depression, with youth between the ages of eighteen and twenty-five being the most frequent victims.[12] People of all ages are suffering from panic, agoraphobia, and social and separation anxiety disorders. The mental health and counseling systems are overloaded with cases. Suicide rates across all age groups have increased exponentially over the past few years, According to *TIME* magazine, they're currently higher than at any time since World War II.[13]

While the culture is pressing in on us externally, our increasingly unstable emotions are weakening us internally. So where do we turn? Where can we find solutions to our panic and anxiety? Can we find a source of strength and courage?

The Most Noble Challenge

The famed German poet Johann Wolfgang von Goethe said: "Things which matter most must never be at the mercy of things which matter least."[14] But are we doing just the opposite? Could it be that most of our anxieties are based in allowing the things that matter least to rule over the things that matter most? In our swirling, busy world, we often allow fear, anxiety, and doubt to rule and dictate our lives. Jesus understands our dilemma and our tendency to worry and fret. Knowing this, He provided one of the most astute solutions ever given.

> *"I say to you, do not worry about your life, what you will eat or what you will drink; nor about your body, what you will put on. Is not life more than food and the body more than clothing? Therefore, do not worry saying, 'What shall we eat? Or 'What shall we drink? Or 'What shall we wear?' ...For after all these things the Gentiles seek. For your heavenly Father knows that you need all these things. But seek first the Kingdom of God and His righteousness, and all these things shall be added to you."* (Matthew 6:25~33)

In the valley of a worry-filled life, Jesus instructs us to quit worrying, start seeking; quit looking around, and start looking up. He is saying the great breakthrough to courage is to "seek first the Kingdom of God!" Noted clinical psychologist and speaker Jordan Peterson has said, "Seeking first the Kingdom of God...is the most profound and noble statement ever made to man."[15]

Jesus, understanding the human condition of fear, worry, and anxiety, is challenging us to seek the highest good, the most noble cause of the universe—the Kingdom of God.

Jesus is proclaiming that if we start off with the goal above all other goals—the Kingdom of God—all other things, things we think we need (job, finances, and family) will be taken care of. He is making an alarming breakthrough statement. Jesus is saying: "Quit stressing over material and financial stuff; God knows you need all these things. But instead, replace anxiety with a new focus on the Kingdom of God. If you make the Kingdom of God your highest aim, I'll make sure that all secondary things will fall into place."

This is the priority of Jesus and the first habit to breakthrough courage: Seek first the Kingdom of God and His righteousness! This is the most profound statement of the New Testament and possibly even in human psychology: Seek the highest and most noble thing. Realign your life around the most majestic goal of the universe and watch what God will do as a result.

The Total Answer to Our Total Need

The Kingdom of God is God's total answer to man's total need. Why is it the *total* answer? Because unlike our world and circumstances, the Kingdom of God is reliable, consistent, and not subject to the whims of cultural and political change. The writer of Hebrews described it as "the unshakable Kingdom" (Hebrews 12:28 MSG).

Jesus came proclaiming and demonstrating a new Kingdom, a new way of living, an answer to life's most difficult questions. One of the most astute thinkers and arguably one of the greatest writers of the twentieth century, H.G. Wells, said: "Why here is the most radical proposal ever presented to the mind of man, the proposal to replace the present world order with God's order, the kingdom of God."[16] Wells was not a Jesus follower, and yet even he understood the revolutionary nature of the Kingdom of God.

The Kingdom of God is an absolute—an absolute answer to every need. True reality is found through the lens of the Kingdom of God.

As a gymnast at the University of Georgia, I was successful and as happy as I understood those things to be at the time. Then, through a severe knee injury that had the potential to end my athletic career, I began to reexamine my life. A friend shared with me about Jesus, His Kingdom, and the new life He offered. I was fascinated. Though satisfied with my outward life, I was dissatisfied with my heart.

I realized my success and happiness depended completely on unreliable, shakable sources, such as whether I was physically able to compete. My happiness was maintained through outward sources that could rapidly change. I needed a breakthrough in my life.

Breakthrough Courage

But then I read in the Bible where Jesus said, "I have come that you might have life and have it more abundantly" (John 10:10b). Abundant life? Now, that was the most radical promise I had ever read. Jesus wasn't talking about a religion or church; He was speaking of a fulfilled life found in Him, not myself. From a life solely driven by outward success and achievement, here was a proposal for inner joy and peace. I couldn't believe that Jesus was offering a joyful, unshakeable life!

So one night in a tiny chapel across the street from the university, I took the plunge, surrendered my life to Jesus and the Kingdom of God—and the adventure began. Over time, the entire trajectory of my life has been altered through following this most radical proposal ever given to humankind: Seek first the Kingdom of God.

Focus on the Primary

If you've ever watched a swim meet, you probably know that a swimmer's "racing start" sets the pace for the whole swim. The way you aim your hips, shoulders, and head as you dive off the blocks into your lane, is the first step to a successful race. One professional swim coach, speaking about the dive off the block, said, "You must channel your energy and focus on a straight line, pressing forward."[17] It's the same with life.

If we have any chance of getting our lives in order, we must get our first priority right. If we get the central hypothesis of life figured out, things fall into place. If you want to live a life of courage over fear, to have a brave heart even in the midst of fear, seek Jesus and His Kingdom.

Confidence is built and fear is driven out when we have the courage to line up all our priorities under God's plan. It is in this growing God-confidence that we become strong and courageous.

Simply, you have two options for what's going to be the primary center for your life: It'll either be you, or Jesus and His Kingdom. I'm challenging you to seek first the first thing—the Kingdom of God. All of life will yield to what you make the center of your universe.

If you get that right, then the secondary things will follow. Aim at the highest, most noble cause of the universe; make this your central priority, and you will experience new strength and courage.

After listening to one of my messages, a young man approached me and said, "I've lived my entire life for myself. But now I see that all my fighting and fuming is because my central core is not aligned with the way of Jesus and the Kingdom of God." This man was getting it. From a life of drug and alcohol addictions to a new lifestyle of following Christ, his life began to radically change—eventually leading to breakthrough.

When you make the King and His Kingdom your priority, God begins to move in power in every area of your life. If you aim at the highest possible good, the things you need to survive and thrive will be close at hand.

Confidence is built and fear is driven out when we have the courage to line up all our priorities under God's Kingdom plan!

What Is the Kingdom of God?

Jesus made the Kingdom of God His central message. He spoke on it more than 100 times. His teaching was designed to show us how to enter and experience the Kingdom of God. His miraculous works illustrated that God's Kingdom had come to earth and we could experience it.

In one of his most famous messages, the Sermon on the Mount, Jesus spoke extensively on the ethics of the Kingdom of God (Matthew 5–7). His parables pointed His disciples to its truth (Matthew 13). In His most well-known prayer, the Lord's Prayer, He told His disciples to ask God for the Kingdom: "Pray...Thy Kingdom come, Thy will be done on Earth as it is in Heaven" (Matthew 6:10).

So what is the Kingdom of God? Many have tried to define it based on philosophy and sociology. German theologian Adolf von Harnack said that the Kingdom of God is a subjective concept—one defined by the human spirit's connection to God.[18] New Testament scholar C.H. Dodd described it as the "wholly other."[19] And Albert Schweitzer, a famous missionary to Africa, defined the Kingdom as an apocalyptic realm to be inaugurated at the end of the age.[20] But none of these definitions express fully the meaning of the Kingdom of God as Jesus defined it.

In the New Testament, the Greek etymology for Kingdom comes from the word *basileia*, where we derive the word basilica or castle, meaning "royal power, dominion, and rule." Theologian George Elton Ladd follows this approach and defines the Kingdom as "a state or monarchy, the head of which is a king; dominion; realm."[21]

The Kingdom of God is the place where Jesus Christ has power, dominion, and rulership. It is the rule and reign of God. Jesus defined the Kingdom of God as both a present and a future reality. Some have termed this "the now and not yet."

When Jesus challenges us to "seek first the Kingdom of God" He is inviting us to make Him the King and Ruler over our lives on Earth as it is in Heaven.

When we seek first the Kingdom of God in the present, we surrender our agendas to His Kingdom, making Jesus the supreme monarch of our life. The Kingdom of God is the place where Christ reigns supreme.

Align Your Life with the DNA of the Kingdom

Humans are aiming creatures. Every person aims for something: fame, wealth, family, religion, or money, to name just a few. But Jesus is giving us a divine command to aim for the highest good in life, the highest purpose for our existence: the Kingdom of God. To make

God the king over our lives, we need to align our values and decisions with the DNA of the Kingdom.

Deoxyribonucleic acid (DNA) is the molecule inside our cells that carries genetic information that dictates our hair color, eye shape, and skin tone, among a myriad other details and quirks. In fact, one biology textbook states that "DNA is the instruction book for life."[22] That same textbook indicates that "[v]irtually every cellular function can be traced back to biological codes…encoded by DNA."[23] DNA allows our cells to replicate and pass our genetic information down to our descendants, just as we received it from our parents and ancestors.

DNA is arguably the most important and powerful molecule in our universe: it forms who we are and provides the mechanism for replication.

Similarly, the DNA of the Kingdom is the instruction book for spiritual and personal flourishing. Aligning our life with the DNA of the Kingdom of God will transform who we are and provide the most effective mechanism for replicating the Kingdom in our family, children, and friends.

You may not know it, but the DNA of the Kingdom of God is what your heart longs for. It is your true nature. This is our original factory setting from God. It's the spiritual code for right living and right relationships.

The Bible says the "Kingdom of God is not eating and drinking but righteousness and peace and joy in the Holy Spirit." So if we align our life with the Kingdom of God, we will discover right relationships, a peaceful heart, and a joyful life. It doesn't get any better than that! (Romans 14:17)

When we ask anyone what it would take to make them happy, some may say riches, some may say success, and others may speak of relationships like marriage and family. They perceive they might find happiness in such outward things, but what they truly mean is best defined in our passage: righteousness, peace, and joy. I've never met anyone who doesn't want righteousness, peace, and joy in some measure.

The Garden of Eden was the first earthly example of the Kingdom of God—Adam and Eve were unashamed, unified, and intimate with God and each other. And God said it was good. When we live with the DNA of the Kingdom, life falls into place. In John 1:3 we read, "All things were made through Him [Christ], and without Him nothing was made that was made." In other words, the stamp of Christ is on everything. His way leads to right relationships, a peaceful heart, and a joyful life.

To live any other way leads to a tangled mess. "Evil" is "live" spelled backward. All sin leads in the opposite direction of the Kingdom of God. To live *against* the Kingdom of God leads to wrong relationships, a fearful heart, and a sorrowful life.

> *You don't break the laws of the Kingdom; the Kingdom breaks you. Sin is anti-life. To live without the Kingdom of God leads to death. Romans 6:23 says that "the wages of sin is death." The cost of sin is death in relationships, death in your body, and death in your future.*

That's why Habit 1 is to seek first the First Thing: the Kingdom of God. This means to discover your natural, authentic, normal way of living as designed by God. The great Church Father Tertullian once said, *"Anima naturalis Christiana,"* meaning "the soul is naturally Christian." [24] You and I were created in the image of God, and that image is best expressed through seeking and finding His Kingdom. Former Assistant Secretary of State A.A. Berle Jr., once said, "No group of human beings, however implemented, has been able to challenge the Great Design."[25] The Great Design is the Kingdom of God.

Just as a DNA molecule consists of two long polynucleotide chains, the Kingdom of God provides us with two core strands for our lives.

HABIT 1

Kingdom DNA Strand 1: Intimacy with God.

You were designed by God for intimacy with Him. God made you to love Him. Our core identity has the imprint of the Kingdom of God upon it. When we choose to surrender our heart to Christ, it is renewed and reborn into a temple of the presence of the King. Jesus even said that being reborn into Christ is how we "enter the Kingdom of God" (John 3:5). When we are seeking to make Jesus the king over our hearts, we are establishing His Kingdom over our lives.

> *Only intimacy with the King and pursuing His Kingdom brings all of life into synergy. The Kingdom of God brings the universe into unity. It's not the Marvel multiverse, but the Kingdom UNIverse, a united strategy of God for all of life and all living things. Thus, when you line up with ultimate life, you are unified with the universe.*

David made the core of his identity intimacy with God. He wrote, "The Lord is my shepherd, I shall not want" (Psalm 23:1). David had found the Kingdom of God through an intimate, life-giving, love relationship with the Shepherd of his soul.

Values flow out of identity. When we discover loving intimacy with Christ, we develop new values—Kingdom values. When our core identity is knowing and loving Christ, our outward lifestyle based on our new priorities begin to align with the universal purpose of life—the Kingdom of God.

With a core identity of intimacy with Christ, our values begin to line up with the Kingdom of God, resulting in inward and outward transformation.

Inward Transformation: Intimacy with God.

- Righteousness in our relationships
- Peace in our heart
- Joy in our attitude

Outward Transformation: New Lifestyle

- New relationships move in the direction of Kingdom values
- Peace becomes the atmosphere of our life
- Joy exudes from us to the world

If you've never surrendered your life to King Jesus and His Kingdom, do it now. This is the first and most important of all the nine habits. I'm not talking about going to church or joining a religion. I'm not talking about implementing some new set of rules and regulations. I'm speaking here about a vital, dynamic love relationship with Jesus Christ. Do you have such a relationship? If you don't have one, you can start one.

> *There is only one throne in the castle of your heart. That throne is either occupied by you or Christ. Jesus is a loving monarch, but He doesn't share His throne. Jesus wants to reign supreme over your life and your relationships.*

Jesus wants to sit on that throne and release His love over your heart. Surrendering your throne to Christ is the first step of becoming a courageous person and developing a brave heart. Jeanne Guyon, in her masterful seventeenth-century book *Experiencing the Depths of Jesus Christ*, described it this way:

> As you speak, "Thy Kingdom come," call upon your
> Lord, the king of glory, to reign in you. Give yourself
> up to God. Give yourself to God so that He may do
> ⌐ur heart what you have so long been a failure in
> do. Acknowledge before Him His right to

26

> ⌐ are, open your heart to Christ and give
> ⌐ou may already consider yourself a
> ⌐rone of your heart to Christ?
> aspirations to Him? Do you

have an intimate—not superficial—heart connection with God? You can pray for His Kingship with a prayer like this:

> *Lord Jesus, I am a sinner. I thank You for dying on the cross for my sins. Thank You for rising from the grave on the third day and conquering sin and death in my life. I surrender the throne of my heart to You. I want an intimate relationship with You. Come take over my heart and empower me to follow and fall in love with You. Today, I want Your Kingdom to come, and Your will be done in every area of my life. Amen.*

This prayer is nothing magical, but if it expresses the desire of your heart, pray it now. Christ will enter your life and through His Holy Spirit begin to renew, refresh, and realign you with the Kingdom of God.

Many people think this prayer to receive Christ is all there is. But there is a second strand to the DNA of the Kingdom.

Kingdom DNA Strand 2: Follow the Greatest Commandment

When asked by the Pharisees, the Biblical experts of Israel at the time, "What is the greatest commandment?" Jesus replied,

> *"Love the Lord your God with all your heart and with all your soul and with all your mind.' This is the first and greatest commandment. And the second is like it: 'Love your neighbor as yourself.' All the Law and the Prophets hang on these two commandments."* (Matthew 22:37–40**)**

Thus, seeking the Kingdom of God first means loving God with all our heart and secondly, loving our neighbors as we love ourselves. Mahatma Gandhi, the great reformer of India and a devout Hindu, has been quoted as saying, "I like your Christ, I do not like your Christians. Your Christians are so unlike your Christ."[27] And isn't that the story of many a non-Christian who has observed the attitudes and manner of Christians? A lot of talk but not much love.

Yes, it is—and it's because most of the time we as Christians are not seeking the Kingdom of God first through following the greatest commandment: loving God with all our heart and loving our neighbor as ourselves.

The Greatest Commandment means we passionately seek God through loving Him with the full engagement of our heart, soul, mind, and strength. But it doesn't end there. The overflow of this love naturally becomes a love for our neighbor. It's not just a "personal relationship with Christ," the catchword for most Christians, but rather a "corporate relationship with Christ" that incorporates the love we exhibit toward others.

> *Habit 1 is learning to love Jesus first and foremost and loving our neighbours as we have grown to love Him. It is with the love of God that we reorient our heart toward our neighbours. We view them from our heart of loving God. His love flows through us to them.*

We learn to view people, especially those we get crossways with, from the perspective of God's love. It's less about correction and more about compassion. It becomes less about setting people right and more about setting people up in the Kingdom way. This then becomes a way for all relationships. We are setting people into the Kingdom of God way: right relationships, peace in their heart, and joy in their lives.

As a pastor and leader in my community, I've often had to take public stands that are viewed as political and controversial. A leader of an Antifa group in our city who had written several negative articles in the local newspaper about me attended a meeting I was hosting. When I saw her, I walked up to her and thanked her for coming and told her what a great writer she was (all that I had read were negative about me, but she *was* a good writer). I then told her that I would enjoy learning more about her perspective through getting coffee sometime. Needless to say she was shocked and speechless.

Loving our neighbor begins with us. It's our responsibility to reach out in love even to those we don't agree with. Jesus was constantly engaged with people who didn't like His message. Through loving our neighbors we can make a positive impact in our community.

Seeking first the Kingdom of God brings all of life and relationship together. It's what we are all searching for; it's what the world is looking for. Can you imagine the impact we would have in our culture and our nation if we all began seeking first the Kingdom of God through the Greatest Commandment?

Get Out of Bed and Seek God's Kingdom

Pedro Arrupe has said,

> Nothing is more practical than finding God, than falling in love in a quite absolute, final way. What you are in love with, what seizes your imagination, will affect everything. It will decide how you will get out of bed in the morning, what you do with your evenings, how you spend your weekends, what you read, whom you know, what breaks your heart, and what amazes you with joy and gratitude. Fall in Love, stay in love, and it will decide everything.[28]

Make the first thing your first thing every day. Wake up in the morning and tune your heart to the key of the Kingdom of God. The Kingdom of God is the homeland of the soul. E. Stanley Jones once said,

> Jesus [and the Kingdom] is the standard note of human living. Everything that tunes to that note catches the music of the spheres; everything that departs from it is discord and torture.[29]

Get out of bed and tune up. Find a quiet spot and seek God to begin each new day. Make the Primary your primary before you do the secondary.

As I shared earlier, I discovered the Kingdom of God as a student and a relationship through Jesus Christ. My dead heart came alive as I gave myself wholeheartedly to Jesus and His Kingdom.

PB&J

I soon found that my heart and life were changing through a love relationship with Jesus. Even as a busy college athlete with very little free time, I started each day seeking the King and His Kingdom. I learned to awaken each morning and set my heart on fire with God's love through reading His Love Letter, the Bible, praying over issues in my life, and journaling what I was learning.

> *My heart came alive as I read the Word of God, prayed, and discovered His plan for my life. I couldn't wait to start each day seeking the Lover of my soul through reading my Bible, praying, and journaling.*

As a new Jesus follower, I started each day doing the first thing first. Guess what happened? All the other things in my life began to line up in a new way. My academics, my dating life, my relationships, and my athletic career were defined by that first thing I did every morning.

It was hard work! For me to rise in the morning and seek the Kingdom meant I had to go to bed earlier. I had to find a new pace for my life. If I had class the next morning at 7:30 a.m., I had to wake up at 5:30 a.m. to seek God. My schedule followed my pursuit.

Before discovering the Kingdom of God, I would party late into the night. When I subordinated my desires and old habits to the new habit of seeking God first thing in the morning, gradually my life began to change. My identity changed. I realized I was a citizen of the Kingdom and a disciple of Jesus. This one habit ignited positive fires in other areas of my life.

I have since termed it "PB&J" meaning not peanut butter and jelly, but as an acronym for Prayer, Bible, and Journal. This is not a formula, but a forming of your life for seeking the Kingdom of God. Since my university days, through ten years on the mission field, and over thirty years of marriage, I have followed this routine every morning.

PB&J is a simple habit. Here's how to it works:

1. **Quiet.** Find a quiet place in the early morning. Sit down, close your eyes, and relax. Ask God to speak to you as you open His Love Letter, the Bible.
2. **Bible.** Open your Bible and read one chapter. If you're new to reading the Bible, begin with the Gospel of John (the emphasis of John's Gospel are the teachings of Jesus, which I believe is the best place to start).
3. **Underline.** Always have a pen in your hand as you read. You will hear God's voice for you through some of the verses you read. When you are drawn to a verse, underline it.
4. **Speak Out.** Read out loud the verse that God is using to speak to you. Read it out loud five or ten times. This will access your brain's language center and build new neural pathways in it.
5. **Journal.** Open your journal and jot down anything you are hearing from God and learning for your life from your Bible reading.
6. **Prayer.** Whatever is on your heart, whatever fears you have, anything—give those to the Lord in prayer. Prayer is simply talking to God and listening for His voice. (More on this later in the book.)

One Day at a Time

A new habit is built incrementally, one day at a time. Start each day seeking first the Kingdom of God. Do the first thing first. When we start each day seeking God and His heart, through His Book, the Bible, it defines the rest of our daily schedule. It changes how we view our relationships, vocation, and the vision of our lives.

You may not even have a vision for your life right now. (That would be the case for most people.) But when you start seeking God, you will find Him; and when you find God, you will find His purpose for your life! You will discover a new identity. You will find new strength and courage. The Bible says,

> *"For I know the plans I have for you," declares the Lord,*
> *"plans to prosper you and not to harm you, plans to give you*
> *hope and a future. Then you will call on me and come and*
> *pray to me, and I will listen to you. You will seek me and find*
> *me when you seek me with all your heart."*
> **(Jeremiah 29:11–13)**

God longs for a relationship with you. He wants to be found by you. The Kingdom of God is your *true* nature. God wants you to be strong and courageous in everything you do. So decide right now to make the First Thing *your* first thing. Breakthrough is coming!

Declaration of Your New Identity (say it ten times):

I am a child of the King!

Questions to Ponder and Journal

1. Have you surrendered your heart to Jesus and His Kingdom? If not, surrender your life to Christ today.

2. Do you have a spot in your home where you can be alone with God without interruption? If not, find one.

3. Starting tomorrow, get up early in the morning and seek first the Kingdom of God. Begin using PB&J for your personal time alone with Him.

If there is no struggle, there is no progress.

Frederick Douglas

He who does not take up his cross and follow after Me is not worthy of Me. He who finds his life will lose it, and he who loses his life for My sake will find it.

Jesus

Matthew 10:38–39

Habit 2
Embrace Hard

By the age of eighteen, Jerzy Gregorek was unemployed, an alcoholic, and a high school dropout. He grew up in Poland under the ruthless communist regime of General Wojciech Jaruzelski.

"Being born into communism is to be born into a kingdom where the King is really bad," Gregorak told a podcaster. "Everyone was oppressed and everyone was depressed....I was smoking three or four packs of cigarettes a day and blacking out daily. I had no hope."[30]

Then, he discovered weightlifting and joined his local fire department. "I had a new routine and a new purpose to my life. I was going to help save people's lives, and it's hard to explain, but I wasn't living just for myself any longer. I became hungry for learning and went back and graduated from high school in my twenties. I quit drinking completely!"[31]

As Gregorak grew to hate what communism was doing to his people, he teamed up with a young, popular priest, Father Jerzy Popiełuszko, who was leading a dissident movement. Following God and fighting communism led to the loss of Gregorak's career and home in Poland.

So, in 1986, he came to America as a political refugee to rebuild his life. He went on to win four world weightlifting championships, setting a world record in the process. In 2000, he and his wife, Aniela, founded the UCLA weightlifting team. Both earned master's degrees in creative writing, and The National Endowment of the Arts awarded Gregorak the Literature Fellowship in 2003.

Gregorak now coaches' celebrities and collegiate and pro athletes, showing them that facing and overcoming hardship is the key to success. He's most famous for saying, "Easy choices, hard life. Hard choices, easy life."[32]

Though it may seem counterintuitive, he's right. On the one hand, easy choices based largely on feelings or immediate gratification often get us into trouble. It's easy to say yes to having sex with the guy or girl we just met, but it's devastating when the relationship doesn't work out and you contract a sexually transmitted disease. It's easy to say yes to purchasing those expensive jeans and the cool shoes to match, but it soon becomes hard when you miss making a car payment because you're short on funds.

On the other hand, hard choices usually involve delayed gratification and develop our character, inner discipline, and good habits, which results in a better life. It's hard to work out each day, but it makes us healthier. It's hard to spend quality time with our kids, but it makes our family stronger.

Habit 2 involves embracing hard—in our decision making, in our relationships, in our setbacks—by believing that this will eventually lead to a better life. Embracing hard is the breakthrough courage to believe God can use struggles to develop the spiritual and emotional sinew that transforms us into brave people!

Life Is Hard

I have several friends who have lost their marriages and the respect of their family due to extramarital affairs. They are now choosing to rebuild their lives through counselling and attending daily accountability classes. They are choosing hard, and it's amazing to observe the transformation they are experiencing.

We've all experienced times when life feels out of control and chaotic. We've all made massive mistakes. Here's the hardcore truth: *Life is hard.* We all get criticized; we all go through betrayal; we all get wounded. This is life. Jesus warned us, "In this life you will have tribulation" (John 16:33).

HABIT 2

Welcome to the real world of affliction and hardship. The crucible that we live in is a world of despair and selfishness. The Apostle John wrote that "the whole world is under the control of the evil one" (1 John 5:19). Satan and his demons control much of the cultural values of our world. None of us are exempt from this reality, and none of us can escape from it. So then the question becomes: How do we deal with it?

Some cope by blaming others. The "Blame Game" implicates our parents, our boss, our spouse, our bad luck, or even God Himself. Some people have a Ph.D. in blaming society for all their misfortune. They blame *anyone* but themselves.

> *I want to challenge you to stop the blame game and develop the aim game by embracing hard, facing your fears, owning your mistakes, and letting God develop inner emotional and spiritual muscle memory of character and power in your life.*

Harry Fosdick once stated: "He who knows no hardships will know no hardihood. He who faces no calamity will need no courage. Mysterious though it is, the characteristics in human nature which we love best grows in a soil with a strong mixture of troubles."[33]

As one who has coached many businessmen, athletes, and religious leaders, I have yet to meet anyone who has made a significant impact on society, built a strong business or church, or developed a strong marriage who hasn't gone down the road of major setbacks and difficulties.

Embracing hard is a new habit that involves breakthrough courage. All of us must face our fears and believe we can experience a breakthrough to reach a new life. No one revels in hardship, but there are those who—through understanding its value—can embrace the transformation of our character that results from dealing with it. God has built us for hardship.

Created for Hard Work

We are built by God for hard work and labor. From the beginning, God created humankind with a job to do. In the Garden of Eden—a picture of the Kingdom of God—He made Adam and Eve rulers and laborers on Earth.

> *God said, "Let Us make man in Our image, according to Our likeness; let them have dominion over the fish of the sea, over the birds of the air, and over the cattle, over all the earth and over every creeping thing that creeps on the earth." So God created man in His own image; in the image of God He created him; male and female He created them. Then God blessed them, and God said to them, "Be fruitful and multiply; fill the earth and subdue it; have dominion over the fish of the sea, over the birds of the air, and over every living thing that moves on the earth."* (Genesis 1:26–28)

God's job description for us is to be fruitful—filling, subduing, and taking dominion over the resources of the earth. In theology, we call this God's "cultural mandate." To have dominion means to partner with the Holy Spirit in exercising the authority of God's love and stewardship to a hurting, needy world. This includes managing people and stewarding resources.

Historically, the cultural mandate of fruitfulness has involved stewarding God's world through building families that develop into communities which build towns that grow into cities, form states, and develop into nations. The cultural mandate includes the research involved in agronomy, physics, biology, and chemistry—leading to inventions in farming, science, sociology, and psychology. Evangelical author Nancy Pearcey writes that "to be fruitful is to develop the entire social world, all the social institutions. It includes the rules and principles that structure those institutions—laws and policies, treaties, and constitutions."[34]

Having spent part of my life on my maternal grandparents' ranch and farm, I know the challenges involved in stewarding people and resources. It's hard work, but it's necessary work. One summer I worked as a "ranch hand" for my grandfather. About a dozen men, including me, worked literally from sunup to sundown managing the operation. Being a hand involved daily sweat, grime, and exhaustion. "Having dominion" involved intentional and intensive labor.

God gave Adam the Garden to tend and work. We also are commanded by God to exponentially multiply and take care of and have dominion over our gardens—our marriages, families, jobs, and callings.

I can testify that the hardest thing I've ever done is raise a family. Liz and I have raised seven children into adulthood. It may be fun to make children, but to raise them with godly character is arduous—and at times, perplexing—labor.

Karen L. Jacob, PhD, program director of a residential treatment program in Boston, encourages people with mental health problems to find employment as part of the healing process. "Working has been shown to help stabilize people struggling with mental health conditions," she said. In her work with people struggling with borderline personality disorder, she said, a critical aspect of recovery involves regular work at a job.[35]

Dr. Sandeep Govil, a psychiatrist at the Saroj Super Specialty Hospital in Delhi, India, found that long periods of idleness lead to increased "anxiety, depression, poor thinking capacity, loss of concentration, and even decline in memory." On the flip side, "there is a strong body of indirect evidence that work is generally good for health and well-being."[36]

The scientific research backs up God's creative cultural mandate: that we were placed on the earth for hard work. We were made to have a purpose in our day. We are healthier when we are working.

But there's more. In the arena of labor, we face obstacles. And it's through facing barriers that we learn the value of overcoming our struggles.

Created to Overcome

God created you with the ability to overcome obstacles. Embracing hardship builds strong people. You have what it takes to overcome the challenges each day brings because God made you to be an overcomer. The entire Bible is a book about overcoming. Jesus challenged all of us as believers not to forget that our world will throw tribulation at us, but through Him we can be overcomers. Jesus said,

> *"These things I have spoken to you, that in Me you may have peace. In the world you will have tribulation; but be of good courage, I have overcome the world."* (John 16:33)

One of the many aspects of Jesus I have grown to appreciate is His constant appeal to reality. Jesus never promises us some ideal, "pie in the sky" life. Rather, He is realistic in His description of life's challenges. In calling us to a higher purpose for our existence, Jesus makes a counterintuitive statement:

> *"Do not think that I came to bring peace on the earth...he who does not take up his cross and follow after Me is not worthy of Me. He who finds his life will lose it, and he who loses his life for My sake will find it."* (Matthew 10:34~39)

In other words, "Hard leads to easy, and death leads to life." Note that Jesus did not say, "Take up your bed and follow Me!" He never promised comfort and ease. The direction of being a brave disciple of the Kingdom of God is the cross.

HABIT 2

Never did Jesus proclaim you would have an easy life. He says that what you are looking for is the authentic life—but such a life comes only through death of self. Death leads to life.

Jesus used the cross as a metaphor for life even before He was crucified. He uses "the cross" as the symbol He wanted His disciples to visualize in following Him.

The Roman cross was the cruelest, most hideous picture of reality Jesus could have used. Nothing in our modern world compares to it. It was a form of capital punishment in which the victim was nailed to a wooden beam until bleeding out, exhaustion, or asphyxiation brought about expiration. It was a slow, torturous death.

In our modern vernacular, Jesus is saying: "Embrace the hardest and most difficult things and follow Me!" Facing this life with strength and courage will be strenuous. He did not come to bring ease and comfort. He is challenging you to take ownership of your destiny by taking up your cross. No one else can do it for you.

Rosa Parks embraced hard. She faced racial segregation head on by refusing to sit in the "blacks only" seating in the back of an Alabama bus on December 1, 1955. Parks went on to write about the event, saying, "The only tired I was tired of was giving in."[37] She stepped out with fearful bravery! Her act of facing, rather than running away from hardship, is considered one of the pivotal acts of the Civil Rights Movement.

As a young girl, Bethany Hamilton loved surfing and dreamed of competing professionally. But at the age of thirteen, a shark bit off her left arm. Instead of giving up, she embraced difficulty and went back to surfing a month after the accident and went on the win a national championship eleven years later.[38]

You could write a whole encyclopedia covering the men and women throughout history who embraced and overcame the "hard" in their lives. If you are going to walk in courage, you will have to face fear and difficulty!

Bring It On

What would happen if, instead of complaining about hardships, we began to welcome them? What kind of transformation would happen within us if we could see that God was using life's hardest circumstances to make us braver, better, stronger people? The Apostle James wrote,

> *Consider it pure joy, my brothers and sisters, whenever you face trials of many kinds, because you know that the testing of your faith produces perseverance. Let perseverance finish its work so that you may be mature and complete, not lacking anything.* (James 1:2–4)

Pure joy? That's a little over the top! But could it be that James was a lot more seasoned than we are (he had already suffered greatly as the brother of Jesus) and had learned one of the great lessons of building a resilient life—embracing hard—can be pure joy when we change our perspective? When we realize that facing trials, embracing hard, and passing tests builds endurance that positively impacts and equips us for every area of life, it can radically alter our perspective. If we can view the purpose of trials as the transformation of our character, we can stop bemoaning our difficulties and start welcoming them. Maybe a new reaction to our problems should be, "Bring it on!"

Frederick Douglass, the former slave and abolitionist leader during the Civil War, once said, "If there is no struggle, there is no progress."[39] He would have known. Even after leading the abolitionist movement for twenty years and helping to emancipate the Southern slaves, he continued to embrace hard: He founded a university, wrote six books, and continued his fight for women's rights.

Elite athletes understand this concept well. They are training for victory; they understand that a medal or trophy cannot be attained without strenuous effort. They rise early, run, lift weights, and watch their diets. They embrace hard. The more they choose it, the more they win.

The Apostle Paul, who would have been familiar with the Olympics in ancient Greece, said the Christian life is a competition against oneself.

> *Do you not know that those who run in a race all run, but one receives the prize? Run in such a way that you may obtain it. And everyone who competes for the prize is temperate in all things. Now they do it to obtain a perishable crown, but we for an imperishable crown. Therefore, I run thus: not with uncertainty. Thus, I fight: not as one who beats the air. But I discipline my body and bring it into subjection, lest, when I have preached to others, I myself should become disqualified.*
> (1 Corinthians 9:24–27)

Notice the training under which Paul has placed himself: "I run...I fight...I discipline my body." The victorious person embraces hard. God created us with the ability to overcome the challenges in life—so stop running away from your problems and giving up on yourself. It's time to embrace the hard. Bring it on.

As I have counseled people in their core development of embracing hard, I have discovered a few tips that have helped them overcome obstacles and build fearful courage into their lives.

Tip 1: Quit Comparing Yourself

Comparison is the worst, isn't it? I would guess that it is one of, if not the main reason, why people give up and run *from* the difficulties in life. Though it's not an emotion, comparison drives all kinds of feelings in us. Often, without even realizing it, we find ourselves thinking about what someone else has said about us, how a different group views us. Comparison is the source of a lot of negativity in our lives.

Researchers Jerry Sauls, Rene Martin, and Ladd Wheeler explain that "comparing the self with others, either intentionally or unintentionally, is a pervasive social phenomenon."[40] Our lives and futures are often shaped by comparing ourselves to others. We find ourselves asking questions like, *What would so-and-so think? If I do this, how will they treat me?* We all do it. Brené Brown comments,

> Comparison is the crush of conformity from one side and competition from another—it's trying to simultaneously fit in and stand out.[41]

To return to the story of Bethany Hamilton: Imagine what would have happened if she had allowed comparison to determine whether she was going to keep surfing. She had one arm; all the other competitors had two. But she didn't allow comparison to dictate her life choices.

Instead of comparing yourself to others, I recommend competing against yourself.

The transition from comparing to competing with myself has been tough for me. All my past athletic experience, especially in gymnastics, required rigorous routines that were judged on a ten-point scale. Thus, I have always battled perfectionism. To compound this during my collegiate career, I was also a certified judge for the United States Gymnastics Association; I judged other gymnasts on the NCAA standards of perfection. So the rigor of learning to stop comparing myself to others hasn't been easy. The question I've learned to ask is not, "Am I successful compared to everyone else?" but rather "Am I the best me that I can be?"

Think of this from another angle. If someone asked you, "How can I be the best person God made me to be?" What would you say? Then look in the mirror and give yourself the same advice. Answer the question for yourself. Quit thinking about what other people think of you. (By the way, a little advice—hardly anyone is thinking about you anyway!) Ask yourself a few questions, like:

- Am I living up to my own standards?

- Am I keeping my promises?
- Am I telling the truth?
- Am I the kind of person I would want to follow?
- In which areas of my life and character do I need to change?

Tip 2: You Are Unique

Be yourself. All the other roles are taken. God made you uniquely, and He expects you to be the person He created. David writes:

> For You formed my inward parts; You covered me in my mother's womb. I will praise You for I am fearfully and wonderfully made; marvelous are Your works. (Psalm 139:13–14)

Before you were born, God formed you for a unique purpose. He knows what you need, and He knows the unique hardships you will encounter. He has given you natural talents and spiritual gifts that will help you accomplish the plan and purpose He has designed for you.

Nick Vujicic was born with tetra-amelia syndrome, a disorder characterized by the absence of arms and legs. His inspiring story is known worldwide. In speaking to a group of kids he said,

> There is no point I believe in my life in saying 'I wish I had arms and legs; I wish I had arms and legs; I wish I had arms and legs.' The first thing I've learned is to be thankful...It's a lie to think you're not worth anything...You go through storms in your life...I may not be able to hold the hand of my wife, but I will hold her heart.[42]

You are growing into the image of God through difficulties. God allowed your unique story of hardship to form you into a person who can overcome! *Hardships are not happening to us but for us.* Hardships, setbacks, and disappointments meld us into the men and women who become courageous and brave. Without difficulties, you are less than the person God desires you to be and become.

Transformation will be unique to each person's personality and calling in life. Each of us carries our own burdens from our past, and some are heavier than others. But you were formed in your mother's womb for a unique mission on the earth.

Tip 3: You Are Hardwired

To become the best you, face conflict and difficulties head on. I will share more on this later, but suffice to say, you have what it takes. *God wired you for the fight.* We might say you are "hardwired." Get it? The Bible says,

> *You, dear children, are from God and have overcome [the world], because the one who is in you is greater than the one who is in the world.* (1 John 4: 4)

The power of the Holy Spirit within you is greater than any earthly power. The power of the universe is alive in your heart; the Kingdom of God is within you. God has made you for the battle. You are hardwired for conflict. The Bible admonishes you to "run with endurance the race that is set before [you]" (Hebrews 12:1). You have what it takes to overcome pain, hardship, and loss. Created in the image of God for the Kingdom of God, it's in your genes to be a fighter.

Those who learn the art of endurance are people who have had tremendous difficulties in their lives. It even seems that the greater the obstacles, the stronger the individual. As a math teacher in San Francisco, Angela Lee Duckworth discovered through her extensive research what makes some inner-city students successful:

> One characteristic emerged as the best predictor of success. It wasn't social intelligence; it wasn't good looks, physical health, and it wasn't IQ. It was grit. Grit is passion and perseverance for very long-term goals. Grit is having stamina. Grit is sticking with your future day in and day out, not just for the week

and not just for the month, but for years. And working hard to make that future a reality. Grit is living your life like a marathon and not a sprint.[43]

Taking up one's cross and following Jesus takes Kingdom grit, Holy Spirit power, and breakthrough courage! It's about surrendering to God's love and power over your life. It's being aware of your shortcomings and going after transformation. It's making the necessary changes day by day and not quitting. It's being consistent—failing and getting back up again.

Stanford University professor Carol Dweck has developed a concept called a "growth mindset." It is the belief that

> the ability to learn is not fixed, that it can change with your effort...that we can learn to believe that failure is not a permanent condition.[44]

You *can* change. With God's power living within you, through a new mindset, you can build a better future. You are not stuck. Sean Achor, in his ground-breaking work in neuroplasticity, writes,

> 90 percent of your long-term happiness is predicted not by the external world, but by the way your brain processes the world. And if we change it, if we change our formula for happiness and success, we can change the way we can then affect reality.[45]

If there is one phrase I hear more than any other as a pastor and counselor, it is, "I can't change. That's just the way I am." I have some choice words I often use in such a context, but suffice to say, no one—and I mean no one—can change anything in his or her life with such a mindset.

The grit it takes to change is found in the building blocks of a new mindset. To look at your character and honestly evaluate it is hard work. A person doesn't just wake up one day with self-control, patience, love, or joy. They must develop a new habit of thinking that builds self-control, patience, love, and joy. Without strength of mind, nothing worthwhile can be accomplished.

> *When we develop mental grit, we create a new reality. If we begin to believe that God can do miracles in our lives and we nurture that mindset, watch out! God's going to do miracles!*

Just recently, a young man who was addicted to crack and meth came to our church. The first time he came, he was not impressed. He told me later that even though he had attended church as a youngster, he was sick of the whole "religious church" thing. But one morning, sitting under a bridge doing drugs, he remembered a message from me on how God can change one's life through embracing hard. He remembered my challenge and said to himself, "Look at me. I'm going nowhere. I'm sick of this life; I'm going to take on hard, stop doing drugs, and go after God!"

And so he did. That was three years ago. Now he has a steady job and he's on the way to a new life. He rewired his thinking with the grit of this new habit.

Tip 4: Focus in a New Direction

To develop the new habit of being a better you, stop looking down, stop looking around, and start looking up! Look up to Christ and His Kingdom and become the best you. The *direction* of your outlook determines your degree of change.

Don't look down. It may make you feel better about yourself, but looking down on those who are less than you in intelligence, talent, or morals isn't going to change *your* life. And in this case, your life is the one that matters. Those people *need your love and help,* but they don't need you or anyone else looking down on them. *Looking down will take you down.*

Don't look around. Don't look at the lives of your peers. They are wonderfully and marvelously made, just as you are, and they have a unique calling for their lives. Cheer them on but don't compare yourself to them.

Look up. Instead of looking at your problems or comparing yourself to others, look up! Focus on Jesus, "the author and perfector" of your life and faith (Hebrews 12:2). He created you. He has a special plan for your life. *Look at Him and live in partnership with Him.* Give Him your struggles and pain. Take your eyes off your hard and fix your gaze on Jesus. Surrender your character, your hopes, and your dreams to Him.

The Apostle Paul, in grappling with the mystery of the character of Christ being formed within him, wrote,

> *I have been crucified with Christ; it is no longer I who live, but Christ lives within me, and the life which I now live in the flesh I live by faith in the Son of God...*
> (Galatians 2:20)

Christ lives within you. Look to Him. Die to self. Crucify your sinful passions, your fears, and your addictions on the cross. Invite Christ to live His life through you.

Looking up to Christ and the cross in the midst of hardship is the key to victory and overcoming struggles in life. We see this throughout the Scriptures. Joseph has to be stripped of his favored position with his father and endure the humiliation of becoming both a slave and a prisoner before God elevated him to a powerful position in Pharaoh's court (Genesis 37). David was driven out of Saul's favor and spent seventeen years running for his life, yet in God's timing, he became the greatest king in Israel's history (1 Samuel 16–23). Saul, the up-and-coming Jewish leader in Jerusalem, was radically converted to Christianity and spent the rest of his life in and out of prison for the sake of the Gospel (Acts 9–28). All of these men were "crucified with Christ," faced difficulties, and allowed the power of God to flow through them even in the most dire of circumstances.

Tip 5: Setbacks Are Setups for a Comeback

It may sound trite, but I believe this saying is true. You can view your setbacks in life from the angle of frustration and blame, or as a setup for God to do a new work in your life. In 2 Timothy 1:7 we read, "For God has not given us a spirit of fear, but of power and of love and of a sound mind." When you begin to believe that you are *not* under the spirit of fear and *not* crushed by your circumstances, but rather have power over fear and power over your life, you can mean it when you say, "Setbacks are setups for a comeback."

You are set up for a comeback! That means that Habit 2, Embracing Hard, is just the beginning of the new brave you. What are the hardships you must face to improve and become the best version of you?

During your new habit of PB&J, write in your journal what you need to face head on. Be specific. Then ask God to fill you with His Spirit and the power to change. These small steps will lead to enormous transformation in your life. Even with fear, take on hard and watch what God will do!

Declaration of Identity (say it ten times):

I will embrace hard in my life! Bring it on. I have what it

takes through the power of God.

HABIT 2

Questions to Ponder and Journal

1. When you hear, "Hard choices, easy life; easy choices, hard life," what does that mean to you?

2. What are the hard things in your life that you need to face?

3. Where and how do you need to face hard things
   - mentally?
   - spiritually?
   - emotionally?
   - vocationally?

Write them all down in your journal and ask God to empower you to change.

Friendship is a much-underestimated aspect of spirituality.

It's every bit as significant as prayer and fasting.

Like the sacramental use of water and bread and wine, friendship takes what's common in human experience and turns it into something holy.

Eugene Peterson

David therefore departed from there and escaped to the cave of Adullam. So when his brothers and all his father's house heard it, they went down there to him. And everyone who was in distress, everyone who was in debt, and everyone who was discontented gathered to him. So he became captain over them. And there were about four hundred men with him.

1 Samuel 22:1–2

Habit 3
Develop Bloodstained Allies

I n November 2013, I finished a seminar at the church I was pastoring at the time—one I had planted with my wife and children in our basement twenty years earlier. Despite many sleepless nights and spiritual obstacles, through the power of the Holy Spirit, the congregation had grown into the thousands.

At the time, I was filled with joy. My newly married daughter and her husband would soon be visiting us for Thanksgiving. It was going to be a wonderful reunion.

As I walked into the lobby, a grim-looking church elder met me and asked me to follow him without explanation. All kinds of thoughts ran wildly through my mind: *Has something happened to my Liz? Are the children okay? A car accident?* I was filled with a foreboding feeling. I asked what was going on, but there was no reply.

In my office, I was met by more church elders. Over the next hour, they explained that I was being placed on a six-month forced "sabbatical." As they laid out their reasons—mainly my autocratic leadership style, I was filled with a combination of anger, frustration, and loneliness. I had not seen this coming. I was shocked to the core of my being!

What have I done to deserve such measures? Who is behind this? All kinds of conspiracy theories went through my head. I was flooded with shame and confusion. Everything I had given my life to in ministry was now under the scrutiny of a few men who had never led or built a church.

Above all else, I was enveloped by fear. Frightened of losing the ministry, losing friendships, and losing the finances to support my large family. At the time, I felt betrayed by men I thought I could trust.

Breakthrough Courage

No number of questions about the elders' conclusions would suffice. I still had Liz and my family in my corner, but a deep sense of betrayal and abandonment erupted within my heart.

When I explained to Liz what had transpired, she was fired up. One thing about my wife: You better have a good explanation for your conclusions, or you'll be in big trouble! (You don't raise seven children who are all strong entrepreneurial leaders without a mom who doesn't take a lot of BS.) I repeated what the elders had said, but she wasn't buying it.

The situation created an existential crisis in our life.

For No Particular Reason

If you have ever seen the movie *Forrest Gump*, you may recall the scene in which Forrest wakes up one morning to find that his beloved Jenny has left him. Just the night before, everything had seemed so idyllic. Their love for each other had been rekindled. And then, just as quickly as it had begun, a taxi drove up and Jenny left.

Do you recall how Forrest dealt with his grief? The next scene shows him sitting in the rocker on the porch of his house, wearing his Nike shoes; then he puts on his red "Bubba Gump" cap and starts running. The film's narration captures it: "That day, for no particular reason, I decided to go for a little run…" Forrest ran and ran and ran, from one coast to the other … five times.

Well, one morning during the sabbatical, I got up early, before the sun had risen, and for no particular reason, I put on my boots and a ball cap and just took a walk. And every day for almost three years straight, I walked and walked and walked. For hours at a time, I walked. I walked and I prayed. I walked and I thought. I walked and I wept.

I would walk for miles as I pondered the confusion and frustration of my predicament. I walked and thought about the mistakes and poor decisions I had made. I thought about people I had hurt and the pride in my heart. I was overwhelmed with a sense of humiliation and shame. I asked God for forgiveness.

On many a sunrise, I wondered how the church was doing in my absence. Since I was not allowed to even visit, I felt disconnected from the people I loved. When God prompted me, I sought out staff I might have offended and repented to them face-to-face. On many a day I knelt in the woods and surrendered afresh my heart and ministry to the Lord.

Fire Pit Time

And then one day, I returned from another long walk to see a couple of men sitting by my fire pit. We greeted each other, and they told me of their prayers for my family and me. They asked how I was doing. Then we just sat by the fire in silence. As we stared at the dancing flames, the presence of God showed up. Like a fog rolling in off the Rockies, the power of God flooded us. I began to weep. They began to weep.

> *They provided no counsel or advice. Just companionship. They had come to love my family and me. They came to enter my shame and pain and accept me in my broken state. There was no judgment, only love.*

As the months passed, it became common to find men sitting out by my fire pit, waiting for me to come home from my long walks. The "fire-pit time" expanded as more men came. Slowly and guardedly, I began to open my heart to them. None of these men had been close friends before the crisis, yet they cared for me. We talked, we laughed, and we wept together. *Over time, our bond grew and our hearts melted together in mutual respect and friendship.*

Jesus saved my soul, but those men rescued my heart. This experience was different from salvation; this was sanctification of my heart through friendship and trust. I found what I had never known I was missing—a covenant of companionship.

Habit 3: Bloodstained allies are people who unconditionally accept you and absolutely won't "cut and run" when life gets hard. All of us need—but few of us have—people in our lives with whom we can be vulnerable and authentic. Those are the people who will build breakthrough courage into us in our darkest times.

During that time, we coined a term: "bloodstained allies." Habit 3 is: Develop some bloodstained allies in your life. What I mean are a few people who will bleed with you, love you, accept you, and watch your back.

I am convinced that I would not be writing this book right now had these men not shown up in my deepest time of shame. As I mentioned in Habit 2, we all have times in life when we have to decide whether to embrace hard or avoid it. In my deepest valley, I chose to embrace the hard. But I didn't choose to embrace it alone. I had Liz; I had my family; and I had bloodstained allies who loved and cared for my heart.

I may never completely understand why the elders did what they did. Likewise, you may not understand the circumstances you have had to endure—a crappy job, a bout with cancer, a failed marriage, etc. But here's what I've learned: If you have bloodstained allies in your life, you can endure virtually anything! Courage comes from companionship.

Covenantal Friendship

Friendship is one of the most undervalued parts of our Christian walk. We have never been taught that friendship is a key part of our growth as people and as Jesus disciples. The men by my fire pit restored my strength and courage. I would argue that without close friends, we cannot have the courage we need for the battles we face in life. Eugene Peterson explains,

> Friendship is a much-underestimated aspect of spirituality. It's every bit as significant as prayer and

fasting. Like the sacramental use of water and bread and wine, friendship takes what's common in human experience and turns it into something holy.[46]

The spirituality of true friendship is forged only in the negative circumstances of difficulty and hardship. Our friendships don't become bloodstained unless something is cutting us. It is in the slashing battles of life that true comrades emerge as common relationships become covenant friendships.

Soldiers who go into battle do so as a unit, as a battalion. Navy SEALs operate as eight-man squads or four-man teams. They lend strength to each other, and they fight for each other as much as they fight for their country. G.K. Chesterton once wrote, "The true soldier fights not because he hates what's in front of him, but because he loves what's behind him."[47] Men who have been in combat will tell you they never could have survived without the other men who fought next to them.

The Demonic Power of Isolation

We are a lonely nation. Most people are isolated in their personal struggles. They feel that no one understands what they are experiencing, so they gut it out in isolation. And they don't do it very well. A reporter once asked Mother Teresa about America and she said, "I have been to many countries and seen much poverty and suffering, but of all the countries I have been to, the poorest one I have been to is America. America suffers the most from the poverty of loneliness."[48]

> *The number one weapon of Satan is not porn, drug addiction, or the misuse of alcohol. The number one strategy of the enemy of our souls is isolation. With almost every suicide note, there is a cry for someone who will understand and love that person.*

Isolation will literally kill you. It is demonically charged. Don't miss what I'm saying: If you don't have any true bloodstained allies in your life, you're set up for a fall.

Not long ago, I was texted by a man who later committed suicide. He left behind a wife and three children. Over the past ten years I have buried two youths who took their own lives. Just last week, I was speaking at a church where a man had committed suicide a week earlier. Men are taking their lives at a record level—the highest since World War II.[49] Behind every suicide is a person desperate for bloodstained allies.

You can choose another way. You weren't made to handle life alone. Marriage can definitely help—but marriage is not enough. You need other men and women of the same gender in your life with whom you can share your inward battles.

God designed us for connection. Children are born with a desire to breast feed and snuggle, skin to skin, with their mothers; that bonding develops the child's brain. Bonding takes place through physical and emotional connection.[50]

Every youngster, male or female, wants to link up with a group of friends. The rise of social media testifies to our mutual longing for connection.

As we grow older, our culture and experience train us to be more independent and self-protective. We quickly learn that people can be hurtful, and relationships are risky. We learn to play relational hide-and-seek. We coil up with our deepest feelings and shame, habitually protecting our heart. It's the way of Adam and Eve in the Garden—running from God and each other.

In my experience with counseling and ministry, most of the men and women who experience extramarital affairs, turn their backs on faith and contemplate suicide are living in isolation. It's not that they are physically alone, but rather they are emotionally, spiritually, and/or mentally closed off from deep, meaningful relationships. They have no one with whom they feel they can share their inner turmoil. And they feel alone because they *are* alone. They have no true, bloodstained allies.

Teamwork

If anyone on the earth didn't need anyone, it would have been Jesus. After all, He *was* God. But even Jesus had men by His side—twelve men He did life with. And among those men He had three core, wholehearted best friends—Peter, James, and John—who went with him to the Mount of Transfiguration (Matthew 17) and the Garden of Gethsemane (Matthew 26:36–46). Jesus needed their presence and strength in His most desperate hours.

One of my favorite scenes in the 1992 movie *Gladiator* is when Maximus—the leader of a band of gladiators—is standing in the massive Roman arena before thousands of bloodthirsty spectators. As the misfit band of slaves stand next to Maximus, fearfully waiting for the incoming chariots to be released, he says, "Whatever comes out of these gates, we have a better chance of survival if we work together. Do you understand? If we stay together, we survive."[51] And survive they did. They won because they fought together as bloodstained allies. Talk about breakthrough courage!

When you see a boxer enter the tunnel headed toward the ring, you'll notice he is always surrounded by his training team. There are trainers, medical personnel, and personal friends following the boxer. Even though he'll have to walk out into the ring alone to face his opponent, he knows there are men and women in his corner supporting him. Many times, I've walked into meetings thick with the heat of disagreement and tension, and I've learned to never go in alone. I always have a bloodstained ally or two with me, *covering my six*.

David in a Cave

It is fascinating to observe how rapidly allegiances can change. The Bible tells us the story of how David, the rising star of Israel, who just weeks earlier had defeated Goliath and killed thousands of Philistines, became a hunted man (1 Samuel 17–22).

King Saul's jealousy of David seeped into the ranks of his army. The axiom is as true today as it was back then: "He who pays the fiddler calls the tune." The men David led in battle while fighting Saul's enemies just days earlier began seeking David's head. But in a dark cave, four hundred other discontented and indebted men rallied to David's side.

> *David therefore departed from there and escaped to the cave of Adullam. So when his brothers and all his father's house heard it, they went down there to him. And everyone who was in distress, everyone who was in debt, and everyone who was discontented gathered to him. So he became captain over them. And there were about four hundred men with him.*
> (1 Samuel 22:1–2)

What a rag-tag group of men! They were more of a gang than an army. But they saved David's heart. They gave David courage in the arena of fear. And over time, David built them into a mighty fighting force. David is considered to be Israel's greatest king, but what should never be forgotten are the "Mighty Men" who fought with him, never quit, and defeated the Philistines, Amalekites, and the army of Saul (2 Samuel 23:8–38). In my book *Worshipper Warrior: A 21-Day Journey into the Dangerous Life of David*, I describe the meaning and fortitude David received from his bloodstained allies.

David had enemies but he also had allies. In the cave of Adullam they rallied to David. I would argue that it was the allies he developed that sustained him when enemies were hunting him down. David was never alone because allies, bloodstained allies rallied to him during his most vulnerable desperate time. They were men who identified with and loved what David stood for—the heart of God.[52]

HABIT 3

Scientific Research

From experience, I will tell you that having bloodstained allies in one's life is one of the keys to experiencing the righteousness, peace, and joy of the Kingdom of God. Having deep friendships that build the DNA of the Kingdom into your heart will stave off depression, fear, and anxiety. And research supports this.

A study from the University of Virginia shows that people see their realities differently when they experience them along with others seeking the same objective. Scientists asked one group of mountain climbers who would be hiking alone to estimate how long it would take to scale the summit, and posed the same question to a second group who would be hiking with someone else. More than 75 percent of the climbers who had a partner predicted it would take them 40 percent less time to reach the summit than those hiking alone.[53]

Bloodstained allies give us the breakthrough courage we don't have, the strength we are lacking, and often, a perspective we never thought of. Men and women who support and love us build up the missing parts of our heart.

No one has everything they need. God created us to need one another. There are fifty-nine "one another" verses in the Bible. Covenantal friendships supply us with the qualities of heart that we need. Solomon understood this when he wrote in Proverbs 18:24, "One who has unreliable friends soon comes to ruin, but there is a friend who sticks closer than a brother." Such friends stick closer than our enemies—and that's how we eventually win the day.

It's amazing what you can accomplish when someone believes in you. Bloodstained allies can save your heart—spiritually and physically! Studies show that when we have people around us, we are braver and healthier. I would argue that we cannot reach our full potential without covenantal friendships. Shawn Achor writes in *Big Potential*:

I believe that there is one main reason why we are seeing elevated rates of anxiety in our schools and unhappiness in the world—a crucial mistake that every major religious tradition and ancient philosopher warned us against. We have been trying to pursue happiness and success by ourselves, in isolation and in competition. We have been told that success is a zero-sum game, and if someone else gets happier you will feel worse in comparison. We've also been told that happiness is a private, personal choice, and that you can't change other people. This leads us to feel disconnected at work, hypercompare on social media, and never feel like we are enough.

This is what I call "small potential"—believing we have to do all this alone. We have been taught to strip others out of our formula for success and happiness. When you choose to be more grateful and positive, that makes other people around you more grateful and positive as well. This creates a virtuous cycle. I felt like something needed to be done to help people realize that scientifically, the only way to achieve our "big potential," is to transform the pursuit of happiness and success from a solitary one to an interconnected one.[54]

You may be literally only *one step away* from reaching your full potential in Christ—and that step lies in developing bloodstained allies who will support you. What we *all* need to enrich and empower our lives are sanctified friendships. *Make this a new habit in your life!* If you are a man, find some men with whom you can be vulnerable. Women, find some women who will care for your soul and love you through the good and bad times. The men by my fire pit saved my heart and changed my life.* The same can happen to you. But you must get serious about your need for it.

Qualities of Bloodstained Allies

I have spoken to men around the nation on the importance of having bloodstained allies in one's life. Few have other men whom they can count as true allies. I know because that was true of me. It was not until I went through the ordeal I mentioned earlier that I discovered the value, healing, and security that come from having deep relationships of vulnerability and love. But not everyone with whom you are in relationship is the kind of person who can become a bloodstained ally.

At The Road, the church I planted and now pastor, we started a 6 a.m. meeting every Tuesday for men that has exploded. We call it "Wholehearted Men," and attendees now number over four hundred. (Yes, you read that right.) As of this writing, men begin lining up at 5:30 a.m. every Tuesday to sit in group of eight around fifty-nine tables in our sanctuary, where they listen to a fifteen-minute message, followed by honest discussion and prayer with their tablemates. These men develop into bloodstained allies. That's why they keep coming. It's not just our messages; it's not just a great breakfast; it's the deep, abiding relationships that are being built. These men eat, study, and bleed together every Tuesday morning. They do this because they love each other.

What qualities must people have to be true bloodstained allies? There are some important ones.

The first step is for you to become a bloodstained ally yourself. You must become the kind of person you would want your own bloodstained ally to be. Be to others what you want others to be to you. It's in being a bloodstained ally that you will discover such people.

The following qualities all stem from being what you desire to receive. When we become vulnerable and honest, it gives others permission to do the same. If you aren't willing to be vulnerable, you will never develop bloodstained allies in your life. Many qualities could be included here, but as the years have passed, I have observed the irreducible minimum of bloodstained alliances. The following are the four qualities I recommend for true covenantal relationships.

Four Essential Qualities of a Bloodstained Ally:

1. **Vulnerability.** The first quality of a bloodstained ally is the willingness to be vulnerable. Brené Brown has said, "Vulnerability is the birthplace of innovation, creativity, and change."[55]. Bloodstained allies must be willing and able to be open, honest, and vulnerable about their own sins and struggles. Vulnerability opens the wound and let's Christ's love and grace come in. This is very difficult. Many people are unwilling to share their shame and failures, but it's the ground of real healing. Until we are willing to share our personal pain and mistakes, we cannot discover the freedom of forgiveness and acceptance. (I will cover this in much greater detail in Habit 6.)

2. **Empathy.** Secondly, empathy is needed. Bloodstained allies are people who have been broken. They understand that all of us carry heart wounds. No one is exempt. They realize that we are all on a journey *together* and healing takes time. Empathy is entering the pain of another. It's seeing the person who is down deep in a well of suffering. The person with sympathy calls for help; the person with empathy is willing to be lowered down into the well and work with the person to find a way out. Empathy is not just recognizing our pain; it's also entering our pain with love.

3. **Power.** Thirdly, we need bloodstained allies who know God's power. These are the ones who have experienced the power of God's Word and Spirit in their own lives. They are convinced that God can save, heal, and deliver *anyone* out of *anything* at *any* time. They must be people who bolster your faith through prayer,

encouragement, and inspiration. They may not have specifically gone through what you're experiencing, but they have seen enough real-life miracles from God that they can believe *with* you for yours.

4. **Endurance.** This sums it all up. A brother or sister who is a bloodstained ally must have what I call, "sticktoitiveness." I've always used it to mean "endurance." You absolutely must have people in your life who won't cut and run when things get messy. And things *will* get messy. Messy is life, and life is messy.

It's interesting to read the last chapter of Romans. Paul concludes his letter to the church in Rome with a flurry of commendations, mentioning more than twenty men and women by name. Paul valued close relationships. He needed bloodstained allies. He uses terms like "fellow workers," "my beloved," "my countryman," and "my fellow prisoners." Paul needed these people in his life, and he loved them.

We need fellow bloodstained allies in our lives. I commend to you this important habit. Find and commit yourself to some bloodstained allies. Such people will provide you with a zest for living well, honesty in times of trouble, and joy in being healed—together.

Declaration of Identity (say it out loud ten times):

I am a bloodstained ally, and I will develop bloodstained allies in my life.

Questions to Ponder and Journal

1. Do you have any bloodstained allies in your life? If so, encourage them to and begin a consistent time of meeting and sharing with you. If not, ask God to guide you to the right people who can become covenantal friends.

2. Set up a time and place for meeting each week.

3. A good starting point might be this book. Study this book together and talk about it.

HABIT 3

*The men who gathered around my fire pit are still my closest friends and comrades. We have experienced many highs and lows for almost a decade, and we have only grown closer with time.

If we want to live and love with our whole hearts, and if we want to engage with the world from a place of worthiness, we have to talk about the things that get in the way—especially shame, fear, and vulnerability.

Dr. Brené Brown

Therefore, since we have this ministry, as we have received mercy, we do not lose heart. But we have renounced the hidden things of shame, not walking in craftiness nor handling the word of God deceitfully, but by manifestation of the truth commending ourselves to every man's conscience in the sight of God.

2 Corinthians 4:1–2

Habit 4
Face the Unmentionables

I am an avid reader of biographies. One person who has profoundly inspired me is Theodore Roosevelt. His story of tragedy and triumph, failure and comeback, is legendary. Many years ago, while reading yet another sketch of his life, I came across a portion of a speech he delivered at So rbonne University in Paris in 1910. This renowned quote is framed in my study:

> It is not the critic who counts, not the man who points out how the strong man stumbles, or where the doer of deeds could have done them better. The credit belongs to the man in the arena, whose face is marred by dust and sweat and blood, who strives valiantly, who errs, who comes up short again and again, because there is no effort without error and shortcoming; but who does actually strive to do the deeds; who knows the great enthusiasms, the great devotions, who spends himself in a worthy cause; who at the best knows in the end the triumph of high achievement, and who at the worst, if he fails, at least he fails while daring greatly, so that his place shall never be with those cold and timid souls who have never known neither victory nor defeat.[56]

Here Roosevelt is providing us a sketch of his own experiences as a leader, but also prophetically challenging us to face error, mistakes, and failure. He was speaking of what every person must grasp—that to be courageous, one must also embrace fear and failure.

Breakthrough Courage

Roosevelt's vulnerability is refreshing. It's not easy to acknowledge defeat. Brené Brown writes, "The courage to be vulnerable is not about winning and losing, it's about the courage to show up when you can't predict or control the outcome."[57]

Everyone fails. Everyone carries shame. Those who can't acknowledge their failures and shame are carrying more than they know. This life, abounding with demons and malevolent people, *will* hurt you. You cannot avoid it. Roosevelt makes a succent point: If you are striving for high achievement in any endeavor, you will have to dare greatly—but with such boldness there will be times of failure. Failure is not inherently good or bad, but it is inevitable.

None of us enjoy admitting our defeats; none of us relish talking about shame, but the counterintuitive nature of vulnerability is that trust is built among bloodstained allies, and your heart is set free through an open spirit.

Habit 4 is the habit of facing the unmentionables of shame and failure. It's in being vulnerable over these areas we hate to talk about that true, authentic healing can take place. Such courage to be vulnerable brings breakthrough into wholehearted living.

Shame Is the Birthplace of Fear

Shame. The word itself sends shudders up and down our emotional spines. No one wants to talk about it; most ignore it; and yet our lives drip with the effects of shame. As a pastor, I often conduct premarital counseling with couples. Whenever I ask about past relationships, most of the time the responses are about heartache, breakups, and betrayals. Shameful relationships and broken promises define many of us. We were made for belonging and love—and when that love is lost, it inevitably leads to grief and heartbreak. Shame is the result. Brené Brown defines it best:

> Shame is basically the fear of being unlovable—it's
> the total opposite of owning our story and feeling

worthy. In fact, the definition of shame that I have developed from my research is: Shame is an intensely painful feeling or experience of believing that we are flawed and therefore unworthy of love and belonging. Shame keeps worthiness away by convincing us that owning our stories will lead to people thinking less of us. Shame is all about fear.[58]

Shame is the seed from which the vine of fear grows. This vine wraps its tendrils around every area of our lives. Shame is all about hiddenness and darkness—those things we just can't tell anyone because if they knew *that* about us, they would reject us, deem us unworthy, and lose respect for us.

> *Shame and fear are Satan's greatest tools to destroy the hearts of men and women! We need our whole heart. We were created to be wholehearted! Shame is the exact opposite of being wholehearted.*

Shame makes us halfhearted. Half alive. The more you hide it, the more it controls you. Shame leaks its poison into our spiritual bloodstream and kills our heart, our passion, and our zeal. (In Habit 9, I will explain more about the power of being wholehearted, but suffice to say for now that if you are constantly weighed down by your past shame, you will live in fear and intimidation and never discover the freedom of living from your whole heart.)

I have found that most people who build their reputations on bluster, bragging, and bullying others are some of the most shame-driven people. They use self-confidence at the expense of others to cover their cocoon of shame.

Run and Hide

Most of us are prone to hiding from our shame and failures. Early in life, we learn to escape from our most uncomfortable experiences. We are terrified of the things that have wounded us the most deeply. Thinking about those failures and dwelling on the shame brings with it the emotions we experienced at the time of the event. Our emotions are important barometers of things that have gone wrong in our lives, and they erupt anew when we recount the pain. No one relishes feelings of anger, humiliation, and sadness. It takes a different kind of courage to face these unmentionables.

When we think about what we've done or what's been done to us, all those buried emotions come raging back. We can't imagine facing those feelings that erupt in our heart. Our most toxic memories enslave us. We feel that out-of-control emotion welling up inside whenever we think about the event. We would just rather run away and hide from them. And that's exactly what most of us do.

I know this because that's my story, too. As I mentioned in the last chapter, when the church elders met with me in my office, I felt trapped and deeply humiliated. I didn't know what to do; I felt lost and confused. The emotions I felt and the loneliness that enveloped my heart at that time also triggered memories of past shame and failure.

Spiritual Breakdown

I was having a spiritual breakdown! Panic enveloped me. My initial reactions were not good. Anger and resentment erupted in my spirit. I walked and talked with God and myself. I relived my mistakes, failures, and sinful actions. Deep-seated feelings of guilt and self-loathing that needed to be honestly dealt with made me feel uncomfortable. I resented myself—for my lack of awareness, for my arrogance and pride.

So I began seeing a counselor—the last resort for many of us. Every week for a year, I met with a man who took pains to understand me and guide me into truth. He listened and then kicked my mental and spiritual butt with wisdom and insight. I had a lot of work to do.

At first, I remember thinking that this counseling stuff was for really messed-up people. I didn't need this! But as the weeks turned into months, we uncovered more buried shame in my life. We mined the caves of my heart forged from childhood to adulthood, and we didn't find gold. Rather, we discovered my "posing style," which I will share about in the final chapter. Going from posing pretension to humble vulnerability was anything but an easy road, and definitely one I had not traveled before.

The Road Less Travelled

Unbeknown to me at the time of my fateful meeting with the elders, God was speaking prophetically to my wife Liz. He had said to her several times, "The road less traveled." As if God might know the future (you think?), He was preparing us for a new journey. As the months passed, He told both of us seven times, sometimes in bizarre ways, that we were on a new journey by repeating that phrase: "the road less traveled." It was comforting to know God was using this to open my heart to a new way of living.

As I took my daily walks, read books, received counseling, and shared my heart with bloodstained allies at my fire pit, I realized I had to confront the demonic strongholds in my life: pride and shame! I can still remember the moment when I was driving on a dirt road on my way to a cabin in the mountains that God told me, "You can either be brave and face your shame, or be a coward and keep running from it!" It was a bombshell revelation.

I stopped the truck on the side of the road and got quiet. Real quiet. I shared my heart with the Lord. In prayer I told Jesus that I felt fear; I felt stupid; I felt like the biggest loser as a leader. It was no exaggeration to say it was humiliating and yet kind of exciting. I knew this was going to be an adventurous new journey.

That day, sitting in my truck on that mountain road, I chose the hard way, the road less traveled. As the poet Robert Frost once wrote:

Breakthrough Courage

I shall be telling this with a sigh

Somewhere ages and ages hence:

Two roads diverged in a wood,

and I— I took the one less traveled by,

And that has made all the difference.[59]

I chose to face my shame, my shortcomings, and my failures. Over the next several years, breakthroughs came as I learned new ways of thinking and healthier ways of dealing with the harsh reality of my shame and failure. I would face it. I would expose it. I would be honest about it.

It was frightening at first. It was like the fear of trying a new move on the high bar in gymnastics; I knew that feeling of trepidation in launching out. Deciding to just go for it took Holy Spirit courage and conviction. To be open with your counselor is one thing; to be open with friends and colleagues is another. Yet it has become easier with time.

Learning to Be Vulnerable

Brené Brown, who has taught me the most about vulnerability and shame, writes,

> If we want to live and love with our whole hearts, and if we want to engage with the world from a place of worthiness, we have to talk about the things that get in the way—especially shame, fear, and vulnerability.[60]

Some psychologists have called this the "swampland of the soul."[61] Let me be clear: I'm all for talking about it and sharing the effects of it, but I'm not about to set up tent and *live* there. That's not God's design. But I am suggesting that Satan and his demons need to be exposed for who and what they are and what they've done to us. When we choose to be vulnerable and honest about our shame, our past hurts, and our humiliations, we are uncovering the strategies of the evil one. In Ephesians 4:14, the Apostle Paul refers to it as their "deceitful scheming;" and in 6:11, the "wiles of the devil." A scheme or wile is a strategy. It is a distinct plan for Satan to deceive us into following his corrupt intentions. Life is not a video game or fairytale; we are in a real war with a real foe. Until we uncover his devices, we cannot be set free from their effects over our hearts.

I would argue that until we are willing to face our shame and failure, with no guarantees of the outcome, we will never become the whole people God created us to be. We will continue to live in fear and bondage. Vulnerability about these dark places of our heart is the only route to new faith, freedom, and belonging.

Own Your Story

All of us have a story to tell. You might not be proud of it, and you might even hate parts of it. But it's your story of God's grace. You can't outfear, outshame, or outfail the long arm of God's love for you! This is why you're reading this book. You long to be stronger and more courageous, and it's in owning your unique story that God is forming within you His plan for your life.

All of us like to tell our stories from the vantage point of success. We also like to forget the regretful situations of the past. But the habit of facing past and present defeats and learning to be open about them with others is the stuff of real courage. It's also the road to new freedom.

The hard work of owning the messes of our story is the act of liberating ourselves from those messes. Getting up after being knocked down is how we cultivate authentic living. This is the way, not just to becoming a Christian, but to becoming a wholehearted Jesus follower.

Jesus is our example. He hung, naked, on a cross—the most humiliating, painful, and shameful thing one could ever do. He was completely exposed for us. But He couldn't finish His task without the shame of the cross. He was crucified for our sin, descended into hell, and rose again from the grave to conquer its power. God calls all of us to put on the Lord Jesus Christ (Romans 13:14) and conquer sin through death to our flesh and embracing His resurrection power in our lives. The writer of Hebrews expresses this so well:

> *Therefore, since we are surrounded by such a great cloud of witnesses, let us throw off everything that hinders and the sin that so easily entangles. And let us run with perseverance the race marked out for us, fixing our eyes on Jesus, the pioneer and perfecter of faith. For the joy set before him he endured the cross, scorning its shame, and sat down at the right hand of the throne of God. Consider him who endured such opposition from sinners, so that you will not grow weary and lose heart.*
> (Hebrews 12:1–3)

Jesus let Himself be completely vulnerable on the cross in order to finish His mission. He was stripped naked, beaten, and exposed to jeering crowds. How can anyone ever be more vulnerable than Christ? May He be our model of vulnerability. Listen: without the shame of the cross, He couldn't have risen from the dead! And so it is with us.

Scripture tells us to "confess our sins to one another and we will be healed" (James 5:16). Mostly our sins are against other people. The Greek term for confessing our sins means to "agree with God" that what we've done is wrong and hurtful. Confession cleanses our hearts. Someone has said confession is good for the soul, but bad for your reputation. It's true. As I've told my story, not everyone has wanted to hear it. But I must remind myself that I'm not sharing it just for them; I'm sharing it because I know there are folks out there who need permission to be vulnerable and honest about *their* stories.

This is not an easy road. Few are willing to face shame and failure. The irony is that whether we are honest about our shame or not, our mind is constantly bombarded with it. If you ask anyone about a past divorce, firing, or failure, they will inevitably talk about broken relationships. It is in the breakups of connections with people that our deepest shame is felt. Rarely do we get fired or go through a divorce based on incompetence. Most of the time, relational issues are our undoing. We can't get along with those around us. This is often related to undealt-with shame that results in relational disconnection.

> *All of us carry guilt and shame; it can either finish us or form us. People who are courageous enough to be vulnerable with God and other people about their shame are those who experience breakthroughs into freedom.*

David was just such a man. David wrote about feeling ashamed, broken, and like a failure in Psalm 31. But David was being the opposite of the prideful; he was releasing the burden of his heart up to God. This is what I so love about him; he took his burdens to the Lord. We see him facing the unmentionables of shame, failure, and sin over and over in his writings. Remember, David is the only person in the Bible who is identified as a "man after God's own heart." He was vulnerable and humble in his cry to the Lord:

David's Honest Vulnerability:

> *Have mercy on me, O Lord, for I am in trouble;*
>
> *My eye wastes away with grief,*
>
> Yes, *my soul and my body!*
>
> *For my life is spent with grief,*
>
> *And my years with sighing;*
>
> *My strength fails because of my iniquity,*
>
> *And my bones waste away.*
>
> *I am a reproach among all my enemies,*
>
> *But especially among my neighbors,*
>
> *And am repulsive to my acquaintances;*
>
> *Those who see me outside flee from me…*

For I hear the slander of many;

Fear is on every side;

While they take counsel together against me,

They scheme to take away my life.

(Psalm 31:9–13

David Makes a Choice to Trust God:

But as for me, I trust in You, O Lord;

I say, "You are my God."

My times are in Your hand;

Deliver me from the hand of my enemies,

And from those who persecute me.

Make Your face shine upon Your servant;

Save me for Your mercies' sake.

Do not let me be ashamed, O Lord, for I have called upon You;

Let the wicked be ashamed;

Let them be silent in the grave.

(Psalm 31:14–17)

This is true breakthrough courage. David, the mighty warrior, the greatest king of Israel, the one who has defeated all his enemies, has come to a fearful place in his life. He is depressed, and anxiety is welling up in his heart. But David faces the unmentionables of his life by being vulnerable and open. This is the breakthrough courage that leads to authentic living. This kind of courage isn't running away from our fear and failures, it's facing them head-on.

Habit 4 is all about courageously confronting the fears we all have about shame and failure. Psychology, neuroscience, and the Bible all show us that people who can face their fears become stronger, more confident people.

I once had a hulk of a man, a bodybuilder who had served as an Army Ranger, tremble before me as I challenged him to confront and be honest about his divorce. At first, he couldn't go there. He wouldn't talk to his new wife about it; I felt he needed to. The pain of betrayal and the risk of being rejected by his new wife was too deep. But as we walked through key Bible passages and he listened to other men's stories of freedom, his heart softened. In partnership with God's power and bloodstained allies, he opened himself to a new vulnerability over his shame. Freedom and joy came as he faced his pain.

Light Shining on our Darkness

All of us carry what I call "dark shame caves" deep within our hearts, hindering us from the fullness of joy. In John's prologue to his gospel, he writes, "The light shines in the darkness and the darkness can never extinguish it" (John 1:5 NLT). Light always takes over darkness. Jesus always smothers demonic oppression. Satan's darkness can never overtake God's light. But darkness exists due to the absence of light.

The darkness of shame and the humiliation of our failures exists in our hearts because we've never allowed God's light to shine into those caves. We live half-hearted lives because we cover up half our hearts! We are captive to our own ignorance. We follow the protocol of "getting saved" and "going to church," but we don't realize that we're missing out on wholehearted living. Wholehearted living is just that: living from your whole heart—acknowledging honestly the "dark shame cave" and brokenness therein.

We need fearful courage from the Holy Spirit to surrender our total hearts to God. Even the shame. Even the failure. This is not a one-time experience, but a new habit. It's a process. It's a lifestyle of repentance. When we invite the light of Christ and the Kingdom of God into the darkness in our life, even the dark shame caves of our heart, He overtakes that cave with the light of His love and grace! Paul understood this when he wrote,

> *Therefore, since we have this ministry, as we have received mercy, we do not lose heart. But we have renounced the hidden things of shame, not walking in craftiness nor handling the word of God deceitfully, but by manifestation of the truth commending ourselves to every man's conscience in the sight of God.* (2 Corinthians 4:1–2)

Paul is addressing those who are about to lose heart, those who are living half-hearted and fractured lives. He is writing to those who want to quit. He dives into the process of freedom by identifying the first step: "we have renounced the hidden things of shame." "Renounce" in Greek means "to speak out, to declare." We renounce shame through forthright acknowledgment of our failures and brokenness to God and others: "by manifestation of the truth commending ourselves to every man's conscience in the sight of God." We must be willing to renounce the shame through vulnerability with other people.

This is the power of bloodstained allies. The ones who gathered around my fire pit shared their deepest wounds because I shared my own. We gave each other permission to be less than the best.

> *We tell each other the stories of our failures, bad decisions—and to be honest, how utterly selfish we truly are! We listen, we care, and there is no judgment, only empathy and love. We give each other grace to be weak through vulnerability concerning our sin and woundedness.*

Real Authenticity

When we take off the armor that has protected our hearts, we enter the arena of authenticity. As Roosevelt said in his speech at the Sorbonne, we become like those "whose face is marred by dust and sweat and blood, who strives valiantly, who errs, who comes up short again and again." We're allowing our broken heart to be revealed.

We're unmasking the hurt and taking the risk to be authentic. And let me tell you, it's not easy! It's dusty, sweaty, and bloody—but when the wound is out there for everyone to see and the hiding is over, grace is released upon your life.

The Apostle Paul explains that we must quit the posing and pretending of religious posturing by "not walking in craftiness nor handling the word of God deceitfully." In other words, don't use religious talk or quote Bible verses to cover up your failure and shame. We must decide that freedom through telling the truth is worth it. We aren't going to pose anymore! We must choose to stop hiding behind the religious veneer of "having it all together." He continues,

> *For it is the God who commanded light to shine out of darkness, who has shone in our hearts to give the light of the knowledge of the glory of God in the face of Jesus Christ.*
> (2 Corinthians 4:6)

Paul instructs us to let the light of Christ shine on our darkness! We don't just renounce the shame verbally; we must allow the light and love of Christ to shine into the darkness. True repentance begins with honesty. In other words, we quit hiding it. End the fear. Face it with the light of Jesus. Bring it to "the face of Jesus"; be honest with Him and share it by faith with others. His light will bestow healing upon your heart. Breakthrough courage yields wholehearted living!

Once, while I was butchering an elk during a hunting trip, I cut my hand with my razor-sharp knife. A snowstorm was rolling in, and in my haste to get back to camp, I forgot about the cut. But the next day, I awoke to searing pain. The cut was beginning to get infected. I had to lance the skin, open the wound back up to the light, and dress it with ointment. The pain subsided as the healing began. And so, it is with our hearts: We must open that invisible, infected heart wound and let God's light shine in so the healing can begin.

Most of us have never truly opened our heart wounds to the light of Christ. We've become professional posers who fake it till we make it. This is the false self, and its effects are crushing.

Jesus Is a Freedom Fighter

Could it be that God is about to bring new joy to your life as you fearfully but courageously face the dark shame caves of your past? Could it be that the weight you have carried all your life is about to be lifted? Jesus said, "With men this is impossible, but with God all things are possible" (Matthew 19:26). Jesus's MO is healing. He came to set the captives free. He takes our bondage and replaces it with liberty. When announcing His mission on the earth, He said,

> *"The Spirit of the Lord is upon Me, Because He has anointed Me... He has sent Me to heal the brokenhearted, To proclaim liberty to the captives And recovery of sight to the blind, To set at liberty those who are oppressed."* (Luke 4:18)

Jesus came as a freedom fighter. He understood His enemy and He came to tear apart Satan's works over us. John said it best: "The reason the Son of God appeared was to destroy the works of the devil" (1 John 3:8). In literally every town Jesus entered during His earthly ministry, His first two tasks were preaching the Kingdom of God and casting out demons. Fully one-third of Jesus' ministry was deliverance from the enemy's work.

Jesus is anointed to heal the broken hearted and liberate the captives and oppressed. This is what He came to do. This is what He wants to do in your life. As we become vulnerable and face our shame and failure, we expose the schemes of the devil and his demons. Freedom comes when we allow the light of Jesus to shine in.

It's not easy to let go of our chains. Those chains have been a part of our lives, sometimes for a long time. It's awkward and uncomfortable to talk about such issues. But now is the time to face the shame and failure with the knowledge and hope of new joy, new love, new grace, and new freedom.

Declaration of Identity (shout it out ten times):

I will face my shame and failures through being

vulnerable with God and people!

Questions to Ponder and Journal

1. Can you identify the shame caves of your heart?

2. Will you take time today to write in your journal about those shame areas that are hindering authenticity in your life?

3. With some trusted bloodstained allies, will you be honest and share about your shame and failures?

Meditation reduces stress. An immediate and long-proven benefit of meditation is reduced stress and a decreased level of cortisol in our brains and bodies.

A 2013 study from the Center of Mind and Brain at UC Davis

This Book of the Law shall not depart from your mouth, but you shall meditate on it day and night, that you may observe to do according to all that is written in it. For then you will make your way prosperous, and then you will have good success.

Joshua 1:8

Habit 5
Eat the Book

L
ast year, my Labrador retriever, Sage, found a prize: a large bone. As I was sitting out by my fire pit working on a sermon, she plopped down beside me with this massive bone that was almost bigger than her and commenced to go through the routine every dog owner knows: shaking it, staring at it, slinging it up in the air, then dragging it to a quiet, solitary place and just chewing—making a lot of low, rumbling, growling sounds of pleasure.

I take delight in my dog's delight. (The fact that she wasn't bugging me to throw one of her saliva-covered tennis balls was delight enough.) But I was further delighted to discover that the words "gnaw" and "growl" are the same as the word Old Testament writers used for "meditate": *hagah* in ancient Hebrew. The prophet Isaiah writes, "As a young lion *growls* [italics mine] over his prey" (Isaiah 31:4) is the same word used for meditation in the Bible.

It's the same word David uses in writing: "Blessed is the man [who]… meditates [on God's law] day and night" (Psalm 1:1–2). In our modern vernacular, when we use the word "meditate," it fits the more cerebral practice of thinking on something in a quiet garden or study. It conjures up the image of a monk in a lotus position, humming.

But Isaiah's imagery is of a growling lion crouched over its dinner. It's Sage devouring a bone: she attacks, she chews, she swallows; she gets the marrow down into her bloodstream. The bone becomes part of her. This kind of chewing and swallowing is the action of metabolizing the protein, the vitamins, the enzymes into one's system.

> *Meditation in its true biblical meaning is to chew on, gnaw, and digest God's Word through spending time on a biblical passage, a truth, with a heart hungry for God. It's metabolizing truth through the intimacy we experience with God in our spiritual life to become part of us and fuel our outer life.*

It might be more helpful to compare "meditate" with another phrase: "eat the book." The Old Testament prophets understood the power of tranquility found in meditating in God's Book. They organized their minds and hearts through metabolizing God's truths and promises in such a way that the idea of consuming The Book entered their vernacular.

Eat the Book

We are told numerous times in the Bible to "eat the book." Ezekiel is told to eat the scroll (Ezekiel 2:9–3:2); Jeremiah was told to eat God's words (Jeremiah 15:16), and on the island of Patmos, John was commanded to eat the book (Revelation 10:8–10). This is the same idea as *hagah*. We are to gnaw, consume, and metabolize God's Word, the Bible, into our system. We eat the Book when we

> Assimilate it, take it into our lives in such a way that it gets metabolized into acts of love, cups of cold water, missions into all the world, healing, and evangelism and justice in Jesus' name.[62]

Habit 5 is the act of getting the Book, the Word of God, into our system.

Eating the Book involves two key elements: meditation and solitude. We cannot experience one without the other. Meditation is about getting quiet and reading the Bible slowly. Very slowly—like eating a fine steak or sipping an exquisite wine, savoring every word, thinking, praying, and asking God to show us something we've never seen or felt before. It's making time in our hectic schedules to eat and drink from the Holy Scriptures in solitude.

Perpetual Unrest

Our world is a restless place. We seem to fear solitude and thoughtfulness. It makes us uneasy to stop and relax. I was once talking to a busy woman who was eaten up by arthritis. She could barely walk because of her many ailments. I asked her if she truly wanted to be healed by God and she answered, "Well of course I do." I asked her if she had ever taken her arthritis to Dr. Isaiah, and with a puzzled look, she said "Who is that?" So I quoted Dr. Isaiah to her,

> *In returning and rest you shall be saved; In quietness and confidence shall be your strength; But you would not.* (Isaiah 30:15)

I told her to slow down and begin each day in solitude with God. I explained PB&J (Habit 1). I explained the meaning of the word *hagah*, and the need to metabolize spiritual truth into her heart and mind. She started following Dr. Isaiah's prescription, and she got increasingly healed. She discovered the curative power of meditation, solitude, and rest.

Author Evelyn Underhill, in explaining the stressful nature of our lives, writes that "we mostly spend our lives conjugating three verbs: to want, to have, to do. Craving, clutching, and fussing over life…We are in perpetual unrest."[63] We have schedules to keep, people to meet, and you know what? We are eaten up with stress, and all the physical and mental maladies that go with it. Dr. McLaughlin of Women's Medical College in Philadelphia says that:

> 65–85 percent of all sickness is rooted in the mental and spiritual. 99 percent of headaches. 75 percent of stomach disorders. 75 percent of asthma and 75 percent of skin diseases.[64]

It is no exaggeration to say that we are too busy to get healed! It's in meditation and solitude that we are healed spiritually, emotionally, and physically through the presence and voice of God.

Elijah had a busy life. Talk about a stressed-out prophet! In one Old Testament story, he has just stood before thousands on Mount Carmel, challenged the prophets of Baal to a showdown, and won a decisive victory over King Ahab. But just as quickly as he reached the top of his game, the evil queen Jezebel put out a fatwa for his head. (You can read the whole story in 1 Kings 18–19.) Elijah literally ran a marathon (more than twenty-five miles as a crow flies), dove into a cave for protection, and commiserated with God over his problems: "I alone am left and now they seek to take my life" (1 Kings 19:10). He was depressed and lonely. But God gave him a lesson for all time.

> *The Lord said, "Go out and stand on the mountain in the presence of the Lord, for the Lord is about to pass by." Then a great and powerful wind tore the mountains apart and shattered the rocks before the Lord, but the Lord was not in the wind. After the wind there was an earthquake, but the Lord was not in the earthquake. After the earthquake came a fire, but the Lord was not in the fire. And after the fire a still small voice.* (1 Kings 19:11–12)

God's MO is most often "a still small voice." Most of the time He doesn't speak to us through noisy people, crowded meetings, or endless problem solving. He comes in a gentle whisper. This is precisely why the great saints who have accomplished the most for the Kingdom of God on Earth have been men and women who, as busy as they were, regularly took time to get quiet and meditate on God's promises.

Martin Luther, the instigator of the Protestant Reformation, translated the Bible into German while sitting alone in the silence of Germany's Wartburg Castle. John Bunyon, who wrote *Pilgrim's Progress*— arguably the greatest Christian book of all time—did so while incarcerated. History was transformed by men and women who either took voluntary time or were forced into solitude and meditation. They heard and saw things they could not hear or see without slowing down.

The Drone

My son Josh has a drone. I'm amazed what he can see with that thing. Once, while driving through the Rockies, he flew it over the nearby mountains and saw things we never could have seen from the valley below. As he flew the drone over a meadow, he came across a herd of mule deer. It was beautiful and breathtaking, giving us the rare privilege of eavesdropping on these majestic animals.

Practicing solitude and meditation is like that. The Holy Spirit leads us into the heights of His heart and mind. We are taken from our busy valleys into the quiet meadows of His love and grace. I would imagine it was during such a quiet time, alone on the hills above Bethlehem, that God inspired David to write his most beloved Psalm:

> *The Lord is my shepherd;*
> *I shall not want.*
> *He makes me to lie down in green pastures;*
> *He leads me beside the still waters.*
> *He restores my soul;*
> *He leads me in the paths of righteousness For His name's sake.*
> *Yea, though I walk through the valley of the shadow of death, I will fear no evil; For You are with me; Your rod and Your staff, they comfort me.*
> *You prepare a table before me in the presence of my enemies; You anoint my head with oil; My cup runs over.*

*Surely goodness and mercy shall follow me All the days of
my life; And I will dwell in the house of the Lord
Forever.*
(Psalm 23)

A restless sea cannot reflect the moon, and God cannot get to an unquiet mind. The Bible says, "Be still and know that I am God" (Psalm 46:10). The opposite is also true. Be *un*still and you won't know God because He can't get to your heart. It's in "still waters" that David found restoration for his soul. It was in such stillness that he was led by the Holy Spirit into "paths of righteousness." It was in stillness that he could navigate the "valley of the shadow of death," fearing no evil. It was in the stillness of his soul that David, even when confronted by enemies, found comfort. The stillness of David's heart enabled him to conclude that "goodness and mercy shall follow me all the days of my life." It is no wonder that Psalm 23 is considered one of the most beloved poems of all time.

I know that many of you doubt God can speak to you that way. You may be so overwhelmed with issues and struggles in your life that slowing down and finding time to seek solitude seems like too big a thing to ask. I get that. One very successful executive told me that to "slow down means I'm missing a deal." I convinced him to just attend our 6 a.m. Wholehearted Men meetings. He finally did, became a Jesus follower, learned about PB&J, and now makes time to be quiet before God every morning. And his business is booming.

The Lord has told us, "You will seek me and find me when you seek me with all your heart" (Jeremiah 29:13). Jesus said, "Seek, and you will find" (Matthew 7:7). We only need a little strength and courage—the same amount you use on earthly matters—to do that. God *wants* to be found by you.

God's Formula for Prosperity

David is the only person in the Bible described as a "man after God's own heart" (1 Samuel 13:14). As a shepherd, he experienced and understood the importance of silence and solitude. In the Psalms, he wrote more than a dozen times about silence. He obviously valued that and meditation. He opens Psalm 1 with these words,

> *Blessed is the one*
> *who does not walk in step with the wicked*
> *or stand in the way that sinners take*
> *or sit in the company of mockers,*
> *but whose delight is in the law of the Lord,*
> *and who meditates on his law day and night... and*
> *whatever he does shall prosper.*
> Psalm 1:1–3

David is exhorting "the blessed" to develop the habit of solitude and meditation. Rather than the loud and raucous world of "the company of mockers," he has found solace in meditating on God's law "day and night." David discovered that prosperity lies in meditation. He understood that true tranquility and joy come from times of intimate focus on the Scriptures.

Joshua, as mentioned earlier, was prone to fear. It was in the context of God's challenge to him to be strong and courageous that he was instructed to learn the value of meditation:

> *This Book of the Law...you shall meditate on it day and night, that you may observe to do according to all that is written in it. For then you will make your way prosperous, and then you will have good success.* (Joshua 1:8)

Of all the instructions God could have given the fearfully courageous Joshua, meditation on the Word of God was what He said would bring prosperity and success. E. Stanley Jones, in his classic work, *Abundant Living*, describes meditation on the Scriptures this way:

The Bible will be self-authenticating to you. It will find you at your deepest depths. You will know that it is inspired, for you will find it inspiring. You will know that God has gone into it, for God comes out of it. It is a revelation, for it reveals. It is an exhaustless mine. You think you have exhausted it, and then you put down the shaft of meditation and strike new veins of rich ore. Your very brain cells will eagerly alert with expectancy.[65]

I have often wondered about the correlations of meditation with success. It does seem that the brain cells are activated in new ways when we enter quiet meditation on God's truth. Have you thought about the fact that of all the important things God could have instructed David and Joshua—the two most successful leaders in the Bible—to do, the common denominator for success and prosperity was meditation! But not just meditation per se, but meditation on God's Word. David and Joshua were instructed to eat the Book for success. More than any other habit, according to the Bible, this is the key to success in our lives.

The Bible clearly tells us that meditation is the primary way we connect with God. Silence and meditation are the means by which we experience wholeness with God. In stillness, we come to deeply know Him. The Sons of Korah, who were musicians and song writers under King David's reign, wrote, "Be still, and know that I am God...The Lord of Hosts is with us; the God of Jacob is our refuge" (Psalm 46:10–11). In stillness we come to know God's heart, His voice, and the peace that is supernatural. In stillness we experience a close, intimate connection with His heart.

When anxiety and fear come, it is through prayer in the quiet meditation of God's Word that we find the peace we desperately long for. Countless studies illustrate the power of solitude and meditation. Across the ideological spectrum, experts agree that meditation and times of quiet can transform our lives.

HABIT 5

Benefits of Meditation

Meditation reduces stress. An immediate and long-proven benefit of meditation is reduced stress and cortisol in our brains and bodies. A study conducted by researchers at the Center of Mind and Brain at the University of California-Davis in 2013 revealed that participants experienced better concentration and lower cortisol levels after weeks of meditation.[66] As a gymnast, I would often take my Bible out on the mat before practice and meditate on it while I stretched. This settled me down for the concentration I needed in my routines.

Meditation boosts memory. Research conducted over the past decade and published by the American Psychological Association has revealed a direct link between meditation and better memory, even under stressful conditions.[67]

Meditation curbs the tendency to overreact in stressful situations. In an early study published by the APA, people who meditated and practiced mindfulness were better able to disengage from emotionally upsetting situations and better able to focus on tasks compared to subjects exposed to the same stimula who had not meditated.[68]

The benefits of beginning each day by taking just a few minutes to meditate on God's Word can have huge ramifications as we navigate an increasingly dangerous world.

Soulitude

I'm not naturally a person who values solitude. I like the busyness of life; I like being needed; I like solving the problems associated with leadership. Therefore, I've had to learn the habit of quiet meditation by necessity. It's grown over time.

When I experienced the meltdown in my ministry life, I discovered this habit in earnest. For four months, I did little more than walk, read, and meditate in silence. I walked alone; I read books;

91

Breakthrough Courage

I meditated on God's Word beside my fire pit. Those long periods of silence provided a deep sense of perspective. As the noise, excitement, and anxiety around and within me dropped off, I realized new aspects of God's love and grace.

> *I had always valued PB&J, but the breakdown at my first church threw me onto a road less travelled, a new journey of seeing the value of solitude and just slowing down enough to listen to God. It was ministry breakdown that led to spiritual breakthrough. I truly found a new place in my heart by facing shame with the vulnerability gained in solitude.*

As I write this, I'm sitting outside on my back patio, Bible open, watching doves, thrashers, and finches dance around our birdfeeders. My cell phone and computer are *not* nearby. The wind is blowing through the trees, and I'm relaxed. No one can reach me but God. This is my morning routine—a time of dialing back the noise and rediscovering my soul. "Soulitude" with God is my new word. My heart rate slows, my breathing becomes rhythmic, and my heart is calmed. I enjoy this respite despite the hectic schedule awaiting me. It's a time for reflection, silence, and hearing God's voice.

> *Trust God from the bottom of your heart; don't try to figure out everything on your own. Listen for God's voice in everything you do, everywhere you go; he's the one who will keep you on track.* (Proverbs 3:5–6 MSG)

My great-grandfather, William Thornton Whitsett, was a poet. My favorite of his many poems is "My Quiet Hours." I've memorized the first two stanzas because he captures the power of refreshing the soul through solitude:

My quiet hours, my quiet hours,

As fall the cool, reviving showers

On Flora's famished, fainting gems

Drooping in languor on their stems,

So, I refresh my life's spent powers

Through quiet hours, through quiet hours.

My quiet hours, my rooms within,

Shut out from day's distracting din,

　　Shut in with books, and thoughts, and Thee,

　　The past, and all futurity;

How clearly seen my highest dowers

Come through the ways of quiet hours.[69]

The culture has trained us to believe that working harder, longer, and faster is the way, even in Christian work. But God is interested in getting things done through our *lives*. The Holy Spirit wants to bring the fullness of the Kingdom of God through us as we partner with Him. Jesus wants to partner with us in the adventurous exchange of His Spirit speaking and guiding us each day in our spheres of influence. This is accomplished through taking time for silence and meditation. This is the challenging habit for the fearfully courageous: eat the book through the practice of solitude and meditation.

Why Is Solitude So Powerful?

It's in silence that we calm our spirit enough to listen. It's in listening that God speaks to our hearts the precious things He cares about for our lives. Jeanne Guyon wrote, "Prayer is melting! Prayer is a dissolving and uplifting of the soul."[70] Silence melts away our self-obsessed thoughts and quiets us enough to listen to God.

It's in taking time to be silent that we refresh our spirit. Even Jesus needed to be alone with His Father. The disciples repeatedly recorded that Jesus would often withdraw to lonely, quiet places (see Matthew 4:1–11; 14:13, 23; 17:1–9; 26:36–46; Mark 1:35; 6:31; Luke 5:16; 6:12). Even after ministering to the "whole town" of

Capernaum, healing the sick and casting out demons well into the evening, we read that "in the morning, having arisen a long time before daylight, He went out and departed to a solitary place, where He prayed" (Mark 1:32–35). Jesus needed the refreshment of a "solitary place" before He could move on to the next town.

Silence detaches us from the demands of our culture. Jan Johnson instructs, "Nothing breaks the power of hurry in our lives like practicing solitude and silence. In the absence of urgent messages and ringing telephones…"[71] Our hearts need to detach from the loud and urgent demands of modern life. Our culture runs on the loud and urgent. But God wants us to run on solitude and rest.

Silence enables our minds and hearts to focus on Jesus. Henri Nouwen writes, "We enter into solitude first of all to meet our Lord and to be with Him and Him alone."[72] At the start of each day, our primary task is to pull away from the undue attention we give to the many people and temptations that assail us and place our focus on Christ and Christ alone. It is in single-minded attention to our Savior that we find refreshment.

Solitude is the place of surrender. It is in solitude each day that we purify our soul from the demands of competition and confusion. We calm our spirit and give our heart over to the Lord. We allow the Spirit to move in our hearts, and the jumbled thoughts, disturbing images, and wild fantasies gradually leave. It takes time to discover true intimacy with God. It takes time to disengage with the false images that distract our minds.

Silent time must be set aside each day—no cell phone, no computer, no noise. It's a time to come before the Lord and enjoy His presence. I believe the beauty of silence must also include meditation on God's Word.

HABIT 5

Meditation: Steps into the Heart of God

This new habit, like all the other habits in this book, takes faith and courage. It takes faith to slow down and get quiet. It takes courage to make time to do it. But anyone can learn the art of hearing God's voice through meditation. Let me propose six easy-to-follow steps:

Step One. Find a quiet place. Don't have your cell phone or any electronic devices nearby. Jeanne Guyon writes, "Outward silence develops inward silence; and outward silence improves inward silence as it begins to take root in your life."[73] Likewise, the Old Testament prophet Hosea writes, "I will lead her into solitude, and there I will speak to her heart" (2:14).

Step Two. Choose a passage of scripture. Let me encourage you to start with Psalm 23. I have personally discovered this poem to be the best for learning how to meditate. Each stanza can stand alone in meaning. Meditate on just one phrase or verse at a time.

Step Three. Read the first line, then pause. "The Lord is my shepherd." Set your mind on Christ. Repeat the line over and over in your mind. Ask the Lord to speak to you as you pause and wait on Him.

Step Four. You are in His presence. Give Him charge of your heart and stay quiet. Guyon comments, "Don't allow your heart to wander. If your mind begins to wander, just turn your attention back again to the inward parts of your being."[74]

Step Five. In this peaceful state, meditate on a word or phrase. Think about it for a few minutes. Don't worry if it's "profound" or basic to your understanding. Remember, this is God's unique message to *you* and *you* only.

Step Six. Write in your journal what God is saying.

Breakthrough Courage

This simple but profound act of faith will transform your life. It has mine. Making time for solitude and meditation is one of the healthiest, most meaningful skills you could ever learn.

HABIT 5

Declaration of Identity (repeat this out loud ten times):

I will make time today to practice silence and meditation.

Questions to Ponder and Journal

1. Go to your quiet place—the place of PB&J—and read Psalm 23. Begin to practice the steps outlined above.

2. As you get revelation from the Holy Spirit, jot down what God is saying to you in your journal.

Gratitude is strongly and consistently associated with greater happiness.

2021 Harvard Study

Give thanks in all circumstances; for this is the will of God in Christ Jesus for you.

The Apostle Paul

1 Thessalonians 5:18

Habit 6
Practice Gratitude

My Grandmother Lucille was an intriguing woman. Born and raised in a small town, she was the daughter of one of the leading educators and poets in North Carolina. We vacationed at her home once or twice a year. I adored her spacious library where I spent much of my time.

Though she grew up as the privileged daughter of a famous father, her life was anything but easy. She married a man, Arnold Holt, who turned out to be an abusive alcoholic. Lucille chose to do something that was considered unforgivable in the religious South of the 1930s and she divorced him.

As a single mother, Lucille was reduced to working in a shoe store. Life was hard, but her effervescent attitude and tireless work ethic made a positive impact on those around her. She later remarried a wonderful man who was twenty years her senior; that man passed away after ten wonderful years of marriage. Afterward, Arnold, now sober, reached out to Lucille and they remarried. They happily spent the last twenty-five years of Arnold's life together. All I ever experienced from my grandmother was absolute joy and a thankful spirit. She literally never talked about her painful past.

Just before she died in 1998 at the age of ninety-one, I interviewed Grandmother Lucille. I was impacted by her charisma and positive outlook and thought it would be interesting to capture on paper some of her maxims about how to live life well before she passed. The following are just a few of her many thoughts:

> *I always take responsibility for my behavior. It is not anyone else's fault.*
> *I take responsibility for all my actions:*

making the wrong friends, making bad decisions.
I find it easier to forgive myself than others.
I don't worry about too many things.
Even at ninety-one years old, I don't have those worry lines
around my eyes.
As you get older, the days need to get shorter and the jobs
easier.
Stay optimistic.
Saying "My Anna," "My Joe," etc. as an endearing term.
It shows love and friendship to the person.
Keep laughing at life. Being all stressed out and worried does no
one any good.
Try being all worried and singing at the same time—
you just can't do it.

My grandmother modeled to our whole family a thankful spirit. She practiced gratitude. Her life had not been easy. She experienced shame, failure, and even had a nervous breakdown after her divorce. But she cultivated gratitude; she learned to "laugh at life" through difficulties. This last line from our interview made quite an impact on me: "Try being all worried and singing at the same time, you just can't do it." Lucille was right. If you're sincere, you *can't* do it.

As the years have passed and I have counseled and worked with all types of people, I have consistently found that those who practice gratitude are healthier, more positive, and better able to adapt to change. Researchers at Harvard University found that "gratitude is strongly and consistently associated with greater happiness."[75]

Gratitude is derived from the Latin word *gratia,* meaning "grace, graciousness, or gratefulness."

Habit 6 is practicing gratitude—or maybe we could say practicing grace.

"Grace" in the Greek carries the meaning of unearned or unmerited favor. It's the kind of love God extends to us for nothing we have done. Thus, the practice of gratitude is the habit of seeing God's grace in a particular situation.

Practicing grace is the habit of organizing our thoughts and faith toward God's love despite negative circumstances. It is seeing good in the bad. It is expecting miracles when everything around us screams of defeat.

Scarcity and Fear

Sometimes I find myself dwelling on what I'm thankful for while simultaneously feeling a deep dread of losing it—a fearful feeling *without* courage. Being married and having children has been a big challenge in this area. I feel so thankful when I meditate on my love for Liz and our seven grown children, but then fear of something bad happening to them erupts inside me. It usually happens when one of our kids or Liz are traveling somewhere without me. I feel a sense of foreboding welling up when I think of life without them—like something horrible is going to happen. My fears revolve around a fatalistic view that something out of my control is going to overtake my life and destroy what I love. It's rooted in fear and a scarcity perspective on life.

Most of us struggle with this scarcity worldview. It perpetuates everything in our culture. The news we listen to is built around it. It pervades business, finance, and our environment. Joel Salatin, a farmer who became famous for his innovations, has had to battle this view in his field of work. He writes,

> We live in a time when most people are obsessed with scarcity. Attend any environmental science class in any university in the world, and at least half of the course will be devoted to scarcity. We're running out of energy, money, minerals, food, water, species, air. In the 1970s many radical environmentalists predicted that we'd run out of oil by the 1980s.[76]

Everywhere we turn, the news pumps out this viewpoint. In the 1970s it concerned Middle Eastern oil; in the 1980s it was the shrinking economy; in the 2000s it was terrorism and safety; in 2020 it was a virus. It can be maddening—and it *is* maddening. But we are all affected by this worldview. Liz has said, "The idea and experience of scarcity started in Genesis 3 when Satan suggested to Eve that she was 'not enough.'" And this has been our dilemma ever since, cascading into our personal lives. We still feel we are "not enough," inadequate, and driven by fear. We daily experience it in the form of thoughts like:

- *You're not thin enough.*
- *You're not tall enough.*
- *You're not pretty or handsome enough.*
- *You're not smart enough.*
- *You're not strong enough*
- *You don't have enough money.*
- *You don't work hard enough.*
- *You don't rest enough.*

I think that's enough! Such statements become justification for living an unfulfilled life. The victimology our leaders and institutions perpetuate trains us to blame others for our problems. Our current culture pumps into us the belief that we aren't responsible for our own lives; we are victims of our race, our looks, our parents, our ethnicity. As a result, our nation is hungry for joy and gratitude.

It takes great courage to maintain the practice of gratitude in a culture of blame. People learning to cultivate joy through the practice of gratitude are the strong ones who have chosen not to succumb to the victimhood and fatalism of our present-day thinking. They are the happy ones. They are the brave ones. They have breakthrough courage.

HABIT 6

The Secret to Peace

Try being thankful while in prison—especially a Roman prison. I have visited Rome and stood in a typical first-century prison. It was nothing like our modern prisons. It was an underground dungeon about fifty feet square with no windows and only a trap door in the ceiling for the guards to throw down one's daily rations. Yet it was under those conditions that the Apostle Paul wrote the most positive, joyful, and thankful letter in the Bible. He had been abandoned by close friends and was facing certain death. Yet his letter to the church in Philippi is a manifesto on the secret to joy. Paul understood the practice of gratitude.

Only 104 verses long, this short treatise mentions "joy," "rejoicing," or "thankfulness" more than twenty times! Paul learned to cultivate joy and gratitude. How did he do it? The lesson we can learn from him is found in four verses, arguably the most powerful in the Bible for breakthrough courage.

> *Be anxious for nothing, but in everything by prayer and supplication, with thanksgiving, let your requests be made known to God; and the peace of God, which surpasses all understanding, will guard your hearts and minds through Christ Jesus.*
>
> *Finally, brethren, whatever things are true, whatever things are noble, whatever things are just, whatever things are pure, whatever things are lovely, whatever things are of good report, if there is any virtue and if there is anything praiseworthy—meditate on these things. The things which you learned and received and heard and saw in me, these do, and the God of peace will be with you.* (Philippians 4:6–9)

He mentions the peace of God twice as he extols the virtue of prayer, meditation, and a thankful spirit. Paul is giving us insight into healthy living through a thankful heart. When I read this passage, I see five lessons that hinge on practicing gratitude.

Paul's Five Lessons on the Secret to Inner Peace

1. Choose not to be anxious and worried
2. Replace your anxiety with prayer
3. Practice gratitude (the hinge)
4. Meditate on positive things
5. Do the right thing

These five lessons are the way of the Kingdom of God in any situation. *Gratitude is the hinge on which all the other lessons mentioned here turn.* Choosing to pray instead of worry hinges on "supplication with thanksgiving." Being grateful is the leverage for orienting your mindset toward noble and righteous thoughts. So, the practice of gratitude is the key to experiencing the peace of God.

I could share hundreds of stories from my life as a missionary, pastor, husband, and father in which being thankful while praying was the hinge for a miracle. Once, I needed $5,100 to fix a broken septic tank at our home, so Liz and I took a walk and prayed. We chose to thank God for all His mighty provisions in our life through the years. We thanked Him for giving us the faith to always give 10 percent of our salary back to the church as a form of gratitude. We thanked Jesus for always meeting our every need. At the end of our prayer time, we didn't have any more money than we'd had before but we did have joyful and peaceful hearts.

A few days later, one of our neighbors knocked at our door and shared that God had recently told her that we needed money. (We had told no one of our need.) She said that God had told her to write a check for $5,100 and give it to us.

We rejoiced! We were already happy and peaceful due to our prayer walk, but the miracle of God speaking to someone else about our problem was exciting.

More Than an Attitude

For years I have heard the phrase "an attitude of gratitude," and I have used the term partly because it has that rhyming jingle to it.

(Speakers like me love such pithy phrases.) Having an attitude is more than a mental orientation, which is important; it must translate into an *action*. It doesn't do us any good to only mentally agree with gratitude. The attitude must also become an action. Let me explain.

I have some friends in business who often talk about having a "success mentality." This is an attitude founded on the premise that your mentality is the basis for how you live. That's awesome. I applaud that attitude; it's certainly better than having a loser mentality. But it seems that in many cases people think that an attitudinal change is all it takes to make a huge change in their business. It's not.

Attitude must be paired with action! It's not the *attitude* only but the *practice* that truly makes a difference. My friends have the right attitude for sure, but in many cases, they haven't learned to practice success. The practice of success would involve such things as the discipline of making a certain number of cold calls each day, knowing one's product, learning to close the deal, etc. Attitudes are nice, but practice is better. Brené Brown, in her extensive research on the *practice* of gratitude writes,

> So, what does a gratitude practice look like? The folks I interviewed talked about keeping gratitude journals, doing daily gratitude meditations or prayers, creating gratitude art, and even stopping during their stressful, busy days to actually say these words out loud: 'I am grateful for…'"[77]

Sounds like the Apostle Paul's letter to the Philippians! This is synchronizing faith, works, prayer and a renewed mind to lead to peace. We cultivate gratitude through the *practice* of gratitude.

Gratitude and Joy

The strong and courageous person develops a habit of cultivating gratitude every day and becomes more joyful as a result. Happiness is never my goal in life, but joy is. As I share the following research on happiness, I want to make it clear that I'm less a "happiness advocate" and more of a "joy advocate"! For the Christ-follower, joy is always our goal. I study positive psychology because the findings that psychology terms "happiness" line up so closely with what the Bible calls "the abundant life" (Matthew 5–7; John 10:10; Philippians 4:8–9).

Shawn Achor, a Harvard professor turned *New York Times* bestselling author and advocate of positive psychology, writes in *The Happiness Advantage*:

> When our brains constantly scan for and focus on the positive, we profit from three of the most important tools available to us: happiness, gratitude, and optimism. The role happiness plays should be obvious—the more you pick up on the positive around you, the better you feel…The second mechanism at work here is gratitude, because the more opportunities for positivity we see, the more grateful we become.[78]

Numerous studies have shown that people who habitually practice gratitude are "more energetic, emotionally intelligent, forgiving, and less likely to be depressed, anxious or lonely."[79] What makes these studies fascinating is the fact that people aren't grateful because they are happier, but rather, that they are happier because they are grateful. Some of those studies show that random volunteers who were trained how to practice gratitude showed significant improvement in their moods and attitudes.[80] Psychology is lining up with Scripture. Paul comments, "Give thanks in all circumstances; for this is the will of God in Christ Jesus for you" (1 Thessalonians 5:18).

We are admonished throughout the Bible to practice gratitude all the time, in everything we do. A sampling would be Psalm 50:23; 100:1–5; 107:1; 118:24; 136:1; Colossians 3:17, 15–20; James 1:17;

Ephesians 1:16; 5:20; Hebrews 12:28; 1 Corinthians 15:10; and 1 Thessalonians 5:16–18. There are more than one hundred Bible passages that speak of practicing gratitude in our lives!

From Skill to Ritual

A consulting group took on what it called the "Three Gratitudes Challenge"—having staff members write down three new things they were grateful for each day for twenty-one days. [81] What happened as a result?

> Some common themes we experienced were feeling calm, reenergized, and more ready to tackle the day; the ability to see things more clearly, feeling grounded, seeing opportunities rather than limitations; and the joy of spreading positivity to others. [82]

Some studies on happiness and gratitude focus on people who practiced and developed skills that led to habits. The thing that had the greatest impact was developing a ritual of a practice of gratitude, done at the same time every day. Some of these rituals included:

- American Express employees set an alarm on their Outlook calendar for 11 a.m. every day to remind themselves to write down three good things.
- Bankers in Hong Kong wrote down their gratitude list every morning before looking at emails.
- CEOs in Africa listed three things they were grateful for at dinner each night with their families. [83]

Making the practice of gratitude into a habit means creating rituals in our life that remind us daily to be thankful. Positive people are joyful people and joyful people tend to be those who have chosen habits of practicing gratitude. They have replaced negative thought patterns (leading to depression and anxiety) with new patterns of gratitude (leading to peace and joy). Such people feel more in control of their lives and express emotions of happiness more frequently.

Is This Realistic?

You might ask, but what about the negative stuff? Isn't this just another "Pollyanna Positive Mental Attitude" trick that turns a blind eye to real problems? Great question. As one who has a natural tendency toward focusing on the negative, I have learned that trying to completely turn off the negative is not fruitful, helpful, or freeing. I must stay realistic to all aspects of my family, job, and personal life if I'm going to live the free authentic wholehearted life. I don't even think it's healthy to *only* stress the positive. As I explained in Habit 4, being vulnerable about our shame and failures is how we get healed. One can't realize the need for healing until they are aware of the problem. Facing failure, shame, and problems with gratitude is the key to becoming an authentic fearfully courageous person. It's the end result of facing the fear with courage when we practice gratitude.

But learning to practice gratitude in the face of real-world problems with deeply debilitating negativity, is a habit that can radically transform your life. It must be more than a mindset or an attitude. It must become a practice in our daily lives. In my life and in countless studies, the practice of gratitude is best expressed in developing rituals of gratitude.

For me, it has been through making gratitude lists, writing in my journal those things I'm thankful for, and praying positive thankful prayers. I have made it a regular part of my life to stop and thank people in my family and at work for all they mean to me. These rituals have contributed to a mindset that has empowered me to make healthier decisions, live with less stress, and accomplish more. It has created an atmosphere of love, generosity, and forgiveness in our family and church.

Just today, after staff meeting, our administrative director was at her desk. I stopped by her desk and thanked her for all she does to make the church run smoothly. I thanked her for editing my blog. It was a simple quick exchange that took two minutes. I believe these easy rituals of practicing gratitude toward people are important in building unity and love in our work relationships.

It's Healthy to Practice Gratitude

Harvard University psychologist David McClelland has found that when students are shown a film designed to inspire feelings of love and caring, their bodies produce more antibodies that protect against disease.[84] In one study in which students were shown a film about Mother Teresa's work in India, even the students who despised her and thought she was a fake showed improved immune function.

Exhibiting love and gratitude toward others also seems to reduce stress hormones and increase the ratios of helper/suppressor T-cells, a key element in healthy immune systems. Though McClelland admits he doesn't know *why* this works in the human body, the evidence suggests that it does.[85]

In his groundbreaking book *Who Gets Sick*, Blair Justice suggests it might be related to the brain's ability to change the way it responds to perceptions.

> The synapses [of the brain] that connect each of our 100 billion neurons with as many as 50,000 other brain cells can be deactivated or enhanced by our experiences. If we see ourselves trapped in a never-changing, gray environment, the synaptic connections may shut down and the release of neurotransmitters may diminish. Conversely, an experience of stimulation increases transmitter release and brings positive changes not only on the molecular but genetic level.[86]

Note the use of the word "experiences." This is more than an attitude; this is a practice. Scientific studies confirm that when hope, gratitude, and love are working in our lives, we are more joyful and healthier. The practice of gratitude stimulates a "transmitter release" leading to "positive changes" at the molecular and genetic levels. I think I hear the words of Jesus here: "Seek first the Kingdom of God and His righteousness (practicing gratitude), and all these things (happiness, health, and joy) shall be added unto you!" The ultimate good leads to optimal health.

Some scientists have called this the "hope habit." Longevity research shows that people who live longer are characterized by a sense of gratitude and hope. The "hope habit" seems to encourage longevity by reducing the effects of stress on the body and turning on self-healing systems."[87] Thinking hopefully by practicing gratitude is the exact opposite of fatalism, fear, and scarcity.

Dr. Louis A. Gottshalk, a psychiatrist at the University of California-Irvine, believes that "spiritual faith helps people lead more hopeful lives and less stressful lives."[88] I know this has been true of my father. There's no doubt that my Grandmother Lucille's optimism impacted him; my father is one of the most positive and joyful men I know. Even while growing up without his biological father, Dad decided to focus on the positive. He is now ninety-two years old and in superb health—mentally, spiritually, and physically. Dad takes a walk each day, spends time reading his Bible, and prays for all his children and grandchildren. Dad lives a life of hope and faith; he practices gratitude.

The new habit of practicing gratitude is going to make you spiritually, emotionally, and physically healthier. Even my Grandmother Lucille, in one of the rare moments when she opened up to me about her "health breakdown" (her language) after the divorce, said that it was only through adopting a new mindset of being positive and thankful that she was healed. She learned the practice of gratitude, and it changed the trajectory of her life. She lived to the ripe age of ninety-five.

So, what about you? Will you release breakthrough courage by starting a new habit of practicing gratitude?

Declaration of Identity (repeat this out loud ten times):

I am grateful for...

Questions to Ponder and Journal:

Put into practice at least one of the following:

- Write down three things you are thankful for in your journal daily.

- Set the alarm on your watch or computer to go off at the same time every day to remind you to stop what you're doing and write down what you are thankful for.

- Take the Gratitude Challenge and write down three things for which you are thankful for twenty-one days.

- Start your day in prayer and meditation over those things or people for which you are grateful.

- Meditate on the scriptures I've cited in this chapter on gratitude.

Live not by lies.

Aleksandr Solzhenitsyn,
The Gulag Archipelago

**If you abide in My word, you are My disciples
indeed. And you shall know the truth, and the
truth shall make you free.**

Jesus

John 8:32

Habit 7
Build a House of Truth

The single-family house is a hallmark of American civilization. A house is an important structure to any family. It is meant to be "permanent"—to remain standing for the indefinite future. It provides shelter and comfort. We could drive through most any small town in America and see old houses built a hundred years ago that are still standing, still providing warmth and protection to families. We've all heard the phrase, "A man's home is his castle," and rightly so. In most cases it's the most important and enduring material thing we own.

Liz and I raised our family in a house built in 1962. Structurally, it is strong. It has weathered blizzards, torrential downpours, and seventy-mile-per-hour winds. At seven thousand feet above sea level, our house has stood strong and steady through the extreme tests of Colorado weather.

Building a properly constructed house is no simple task. Ask any contractor. It takes architectural knowledge, careful planning, and solid materials.

Building a house of truth is similar: It takes copious research, a willingness to be challenged, and the humility to admit error. Building a house of truth is a mindset, a routine, and a habit that we must develop. One might say breakthrough courage is needed to do it.

The Book of Proverbs in the Old Testament, one of the oldest pieces of literature on truth, was written by Solomon, the son of King David. Considered by most scholars to be the wisest man in the world at the time, he wrote, "Through wisdom a house is built, and by understanding it is established; by knowledge the rooms are filled"

(Proverbs 24:3–4). Solomon is metaphorically comparing the construction of a house to a life of attaining truth for our lives.

Habit 7 involves building a house of truth in your life. To do this in a culture of unbelief, deception, and fake news is no easy task. Fear of facts inundates our mainstream media and political orthodoxy. To develop a habit of building truth into your life takes uncommon courage.

For some of you, this might even be the most frightening of all the habits. To be willing to challenge the American cultural orthodoxy of science, philosophy, politics, and religion induces fear. It takes fearful bravery to build this new habit.

Building a House of Truth Sets You Free

Learning the art of courageous truth seeking will break the power of fear and set you free. Being a truth seeker builds a house of truth, and a house of truth brings new liberty! Courage is developed when we know and live by truth. Building a house of truth means discovering it and adjusting our lives to abide by it. Jesus said,

"If you abide in My word, you are My disciples indeed. And you shall know the truth, and the truth shall make you free."
(John 8:31–32)

Seeking truth begins with abiding in Kingdom principles. To start each day seeking the Kingdom of God through reading the Bible is the first great habit. It is from such a discipline that we establish a baseline for judging all other truths.

There is great freedom when we know we are living by truth. Such freedom gives us strength and courage when people oppose us. And yes, we are often opposed. Becoming a seeker of truth is unsettling at first, but it becomes liberating as the new truth structure of your life is built and reinforced. Deep peace settles into our minds and hearts when we've done the research and found truth.

But how do we discover truth?

114

HABIT 7

What Is Truth?

The question of how truth is defined has been the philosopher's quest since the beginning of civilization. Even Pilate, in questioning Jesus at His trial, asked, "What is truth?" (John 18:38). Defining truth is perplexing to even the most intelligent, and every noted philosopher has had a different definition. The definition of truth in Harper's Bible Dictionary says, "God is truth," so as I look at all the academic disciplines that grapple with truth, this is my starting point. But I don't end there. In classifying a definition for truth, I will use this:

> Truth is that which conforms with fact or reality. Truth is not determined by personal feelings, popular vote, scientific consensus, or any human court of appeal. Truth simply is what is and is anchored in the God who created and sustains the universe.[89]

Even the works of two of the leading philosophers of the twentieth century, G.E. Moore and Bertrand Russell—not Christians—line up partially with the above definition. They are famous for the Correspondence Theory, which simply states that "[truth is] what we believe or say is true if it corresponds to the way things actually are—to the facts."[90] In other words, truth must line up with reality.

Let me propose five building blocks for constructing a house of truth in your life.

Building Block 1: The Bible Is Our Foundation

Liz and I have lived in our house for more than twenty-five years and completed three remodels, increasing the size from 12 square feet to almost five thousand. It was gradual over twenty years, but each time, we built it up and out—all based on the same sixty-year-old foundation, which has proven to be enduring, strong, and secure.

Jesus used a house foundation as a metaphor at the conclusion of His Sermon on the Mount (Matthew 5–7) to illustrate how wisdom is built in one's life. He said that when we choose to follow the way of the Kingdom of God, we are building our house on the rock of truth:

> *"Therefore, whoever hears these sayings of mine, I will liken him to a wise man who built his house on the rock: and the rain descended, the floods came, and the winds blew and beat on that house; and it did not fall, for it was founded on the rock."* (Matthew 7:24–25)

So, if we are going to build a life based on the rock of truth, we must start with a strong foundation. There is no stronger foundation of truth than the Bible. For centuries, some of the world's greatest musicians, leaders, and evangelists have looked to it for inspiration, for comfort, and to make sense of the world.

Johann Sebastian Bach, often considered the greatest musician and composer of all time, faithfully read and drew inspiration from the Bible. He saw it as foundational for his music. Bach jotted a note in his personal Bible in the margins of 1 Chronicles 25, "This chapter is the true foundation of all God-pleasing music." One scholar indicated that Bach was "a Christian who lived with the Bible."[91] Not surprisingly, much of Bach's music was inspired by Biblical truths.

Abraham Lincoln, often considered the greatest American president, said the Bible "is the best gift God has given to man. All the good the Savior gave to the world was communicated through this book."[92] And Billy Graham, the greatest evangelist of the twentieth century, said, "The Bible is God's book of promises, and unlike the books of men, it does not change or get out of date."[93] The Bible has withstood the test of time and has been a foundation of truth for men and women for centuries. And it should be your foundation of truth as well.

All of us will experience storms of lies, floods of falsehoods, and the winds of shifting culture. Today's news is full of disconcerting events and disorienting opinions. How shall we measure their validity? By building a strong solid foundation for our houses of truth and living in them. A house with a strong foundation of truth will stand the test of fake science, political lies, and misinformation.

This is the power of beginning each day with PB&J (Habit 1). This is the reason we can embrace hard things (Habit 2). Building a house of truth from the Scriptures empowers us to develop bloodstained allies (Habit 3) and face our shame and failures (Habit 4). This is the strength gained through eating the Book (Habit 5). When we begin each day engaging with the Bible and being led by it, we discover truth to live by.

Jesus said, "I am the way and the truth and life, no one comes to the Father but through Me" (John 14:6). The Jesus way is always in the direction of truth and life. It isn't easy to follow His way, but it's the only way to find the Father. Lay the proper foundation. It will set you free and it will build up your mind and heart with strength and courage.

Building Block 2: Follow Time-Tested Precedents

Stare decisis is a Latin term meaning "to stand by things already decided." This phrase represents one of the most important principles of the American legal system, meaning that "courts and judges should honor 'precedent'—or the decisions, rulings, and opinions from prior cases."[94] The facts don't have to be exactly the same for legal "precedent" to control or dictate the outcome of a new case. In the legal system, precedent not only encourages stability in the law, but it also gives new judges and lawyers the benefit of the considered judgment of the hundreds of jurists who came before.

This legal concept is instructive and analogous to how Christians should decide which theology and historical accounts to follow. I first lean on the time-tested precedent of God's Word (i.e., the Bible) and then church history. I believe in the precedents set by theologians of the past who have grappled with the same issues I do. I fully realize that they sometimes had disagreements and mistakes, but the theology and principles that have survived for centuries deserve respect—much more respect than the ideas fresh out of the stream of present culture.

Recently, I found myself answering questions from several friends about a controversial cultural issue related to comments a very famous pastor had made in favor of a particular viewpoint that was consistent with popular culture but inconsistent with the Bible and world history. His theological perspective had changed as culture changed. Here is what I wrote about that:

> *It all relates to assumptions and precedent. I look at the precedent of the Bible and church history. On such questions, I have two markers for decision making: I first start with the Bible, which is inerrant and infallible. I also believe in looking at Christian history for guidance. When Pastor _____ and others like him open the Word, they interpret [it] based on the changing times and circumstances in society, whereas I try to practice the opposite approach: I assume that the origin of truth and authority comes from the Bible, and I adjust my view of the culture based on biblical truth and authority. But not just that, I also make decisions based on the precedent of two thousand years of church history. I put great weight on what historians and theologians have taught. I care about and lean on the biblical interpretation of men like Augustine, Luther, and Calvin—all whose theology is time-tested.*

Sometimes we can think that the past twenty-five or thirty years contain the epitome of knowledge—especially with the recent advancements in technology, science, and communication. But nothing could be further from the truth. Just a quick look back at history tells us that leaning too heavily on current cultural values is dangerous. For example, if we were purely following culture in the 1960s, we would have supported banning interracial marriage. If we were purely following culture in the 1800s, we would have supported women being treated like property. Yet, if we were following the Bible and church history instead, we would know that the Apostle Paul told us: "There is no Jew or Greek, slave or free, male or female; you are all one in Christ Jesus" (Galatians 3:28).

On the flip side, instead of looking to culture as our guide, we should look to principles and precedent that have withstood the test of time. For example, there is a knowledge base that has guided and continues to guide most successful cultures—and that knowledge base is largely inspired by Old and New Testament principles, not current cultural values.

> *Believe all truth is God's truth, wherever it comes from. All successful cultures follow biblical principles, even if they aren't expressly "Christian."*

For example, almost all cultures hold that murder, hatred, lying, cheating, and infidelity are wrong. And most cultures affirm love, beauty, honesty, sacrifice, and commitment. Historian Nial Ferguson affirmed this principle when he wrote, "The dead outnumber the living fourteen to one, and we ignore the accumulated experience of such a large majority at our peril."[95]

The American church of the twenty-first century faces a predicament. The willingness of pastors to accommodate culture rather than confront it with God's truth has weakened it. Not unlike the Lutheran Church in Germany during the time of Hitler in the 1930s and 1940s, who stood idly by as Jews were exterminated, the American church is unwilling to confront sin in society for fear of losing popularity or upsetting the status quo. The result is a weakened pastorate and a demoralized body.

New York Times bestselling author Eric Metaxas, has written about the life of Lutheran pastor Dietrich Bonhoeffer and his powerful opposition to the Nazi regime, as well as William Wilberforce's twenty-five-year fight to free the slaves in England as examples of how we should confront culture today:

> We pretend we would have spoken out for the Jews
> in Bonhoeffer's day, or that we would have spoken
> against the slave trade in Wilberforce's day, but are we
> speaking out today on the issues that are no less
> important to God in our time? If not, we are
> deceiving ourselves.[96]

So, when you are presented with a moral dilemma or a temptation to cave to culture, look first to the Bible for guidance. If the Bible doesn't provide an exact answer, look to the theology and history that have guided others on similar issues. The answer will be there, even if it isn't necessarily the one you want to read or hear.

Building Block 3: Seek the Uncomfortable Truth and Be Skeptical

While Liz and I were living in Tokyo many years ago, we were excited about the birth of our first child. Like many young couples, we were taking all our cues on labor from the conventional knowledge of doctors and health professionals, and we followed what we were told. We trusted the "medical experts"—and ended up having a highly interventionist C-section. From being told we must have an induced labor to finding out later that our doctor only told us that because he needed to get to a golf tournament before our due date, we joined the 30 percent of parents whose children were delivered by C-section in the 1980s.

After a few months of introspection and research, we figured out that the doctor likely did not conduct the delivery properly. It took us years of further reading, study, and research to better understand that money was possibly a perverse incentive to promote C-sections (NPR reported on this phenomenon in 2013).

When we were expecting our second child, we were living in Okinawa. We told our American doctor about our concerns about the previous delivery and discussed other options we had researched related to vaginal birth after C-section (VBAC). But his delivery practices were the same as the Tokyo doctor's. He dismissed our concerns and proposals. How dare we challenge his knowledge and authority as a doctor? So we left him and followed a healthy birth plan of our own making, based in science and common sense. And we had a successful, problem-free birth.

It's hard to think for ourselves. We all tend to be intellectually lazy. We simply parrot what we've heard from others, but rarely know why we believe what we believe. That's why we like political parties: They tell us how to think about issues, and we dutifully follow. After all, we've been screamed at from the mainstream media to "follow the experts." That's why we like to put our trust in people with letters after their name: M.D., Ph.D, MA, etc.

Building and seeking truth involves work and effort. It means reading, listening, and researching. And often, it challenges us to go against conventional knowledge—and sometimes even against our own ideology.

We need to be willing to go against cultural thinking and our own preconceived views. Build a habit of seeking truth instead of following the crowd. Truth can be hidden and not easily discerned. You must seek it. Truth can also be uncomfortable; it will tell us what we *need* to hear, not merely what we *want* to hear.

Learning to be a truth seeker is one of the great lessons of a brave life. As we seek out truth, we'll be amazed how much misinformation is out there. It can be uncomfortable. The German philosopher Friedrich Nietzsche is quoted as saying,

> The strength of a person's spirit would…be measured by how much "truth" he could tolerate, or more precisely, to what extent he needs to have it diluted, disguised, sweetened, muted, falsified.[97]

In his famous book *Animal Farm*, George Orwell made a similar statement: "If liberty means anything at all, it means the right to tell people what they do not want to hear."[98]

Breakthrough Courage

We will often settle for believing in the comfortable lie rather than seeking the uncomfortable truth.

Some have said that people are like sheep in our tendency to blindly follow what we're told—derisively using the term "sheeple." Sheep are interesting. They have a strong instinct to follow the sheep directly in front of them. They're not skeptical or discerning, and will follow each other to their own doom. One website dedicated to facts about the animal states that "sheep will follow each other to slaughter."[99]

We as humans have a lot of these "sheeplike" qualities. We like to go along to get along—even if it leads to our own destruction or pain. We have very little discernment and will follow whatever "experts" tell us to do.

The COVID pandemic is a prime example of this kind of behavior. At the beginning of the lockdowns, toilet paper was flying off the shelves at a record pace. Why? Because of mass panic about what might happen next.

During the lockdowns, most people simply did what the government and medical "experts" told us to do. We stayed home. We kept our kids out of school. We stopped seeing each other socially. We stopped going to the office. Like sheep on their way to the slaughter, we followed the "experts" straight into depression, isolation, and financial insolvency.

Few listened to the medical researchers who were sounding the alarm from the beginning about the social and medical dangers of lockdowns. Many of us didn't want to follow these skeptics because they weren't "mainstream experts."

When we seek truth and learn new things within certain disciplines, we build on that knowledge when the next challenge arrives. It was from our base of knowledge built during our first pregnancy (and subsequently, six more) that Liz and I learned truths about other areas of health. That practice made us more aware of the mainstream healthcare industry and its tendency to spread ideas (lies) that are not always based in true science. This, in turn, prepared us for COVID.

So when the lockdowns came, we and a team of medical experts at our church went into hyperdrive—studying what the virus was, where it came from, and what truly healed people from it. We learned from other viral experts and doctors of immunology a different narrative than the one being spread on the news.

We realized that the lockdowns encouraged by both political parties were not based on the discipline of evidence-based medicine or rigorous scientific research. Instead, medical and political authorities manufactured "scientific consensus" by cherry-picking data to support their biased and predetermined policies.

Our research led us to a greater understanding of the body's power to heal itself. This in turn empowered us to realize that the draconian measures our government and healthcare industry were taking were not only unhealthy, but in most cases, harmful.

Recently, researchers at John Hopkins University vindicated the skeptics and indicted the mainstream experts, revealing that "lockdowns have done little to reduce COVID deaths but have had 'devastating effects' on economies and numerous social ills."[100]

The knowledge we built during COVID led us to better understand the importance of the foods we eat, the need for certain vitamins, and the restorative power of our God-given immune system. One of our members, a retired Army nurse who became a health researcher, Pamela Holloway, cocreated the first holistic peer-reviewed protocol for COVID, published by the Academy of Comprehensive Integrative Medicine, and then implemented it through our church as a ministry.[101] She helped people heal themselves through following God's Kingdom way—physically and spiritually—encouraging them not only to utilize her protocol, but also to how to seek the Lord and hear His voice.

Pamela then went on to create another website, Radical Resilience + Health, to set the foundation that allows people to maintain physical, emotional, mental, and spiritual resilience in their lives.[102] She built a Kingdom culture of health into our church that literally healed more than three thousand people across our county during the COVID scare!

In his farewell speech—one of the most important American speeches of the twentieth century—President Dwight D. Eisenhower warned Americans against blindly trusting scientific policy setters:

> The potential for the rise of misplaced power exists and will persist...We must never let the weight of this combination endanger our liberties or democratic processes. In this revolution, research has become central; it has also become more formalized, complex, and costly. A steadily increasing share is conducted for, by, or at the direction of the Federal government...The prospect of domination of the nation's scholars by Federal employment, project allocations, and the power of money is ever present and is gravely to be regarded. We must...be alert to the...danger that public policy could itself become the captive of a scientifically technological elite.[103]

As a former general, Eisenhower understood better than most the federal government's tendency to abandon real truth for quick-fix, money-making enterprises. He prophesied of a growing network of agencies that would dominate education, science, and research.

Build a house of truth by staying skeptical, seeking the uncomfortable truth, and rejecting the comfortable lie.

Building Block 4: Learn the Art of Listening

We live in a country full of ideological echo chambers in which we consume only content that reinforces what we *already* believe and think. With the rise of the internet and social media, it's getting worse, not better. According to National Public Radio, Google, Facebook, Instagram, and X all use algorithms that "steer us toward articles that reflect our own ideological preferences, and search results usually echo what we already know and like."[104] These algorithms, based on our reading and website searches, quickly discern our ideology, and supply more data to support our viewpoints. We end up seeing and hearing perspectives that align only with our views, thus eliminating any counterarguments.

Listening to people with whom we disagree is a forgotten art. It's very hard, but it's necessary to build a library of information not based solely on single viewpoints. I have made it a habit to listen to those with whom I vehemently disagree. I have met with political and religious leaders with whom I have very little in common because I want to understand their perspective. This has helped me have compassion and love in my heart rather than acrimony or distant hatred.

I think this mindset was built into me through my mom and dad. Both were liberal Democrats who loved and supported Dr. Martin Luther King Jr. and the Civil Rights Movement. My dad even marched at Dr. King's funeral.

I grew up in the Jim Crow era, hearing the stories and experiencing the racism of the South. I was in middle school when South Carolina fully integrated the educational system in 1970. Because of things I said in defence of my black friends, my classmates called me a "n***** lover.". But at home, every night I heard the stories of Dr. King and his comrades as they marched for their rights and faced ridicule. My dad stood up to the governor of South Carolina, going to the state capitol with a group of black leaders who petitioned for the Confederate flag to be taken down in Columbia. I realized at an early age that segregation—whether racial or even ideological—leads to hatred, dehumanization, and disunity, and were reinforced by keeping white and black people separate and afar from each other.

If we want to be more compassionate, more loving, and more knowledgeable, then listen to the liberal neighbour with whom you disagree; listen to your conservative uncle whose views don't line up with yours; listen to podcasts with different ideological perspectives or read newspapers you don't normally read.

As a truth seeker building a house of truth, I want to encourage you to listen to and understand people who don't agree with you. Jesus commanded us to love our neighbors—not just the ones who believes what we believe or vote the way we vote. As Brené Brown tells us: "It's hard to hate people up close."[105]

A newspaper columnist eloquently wrote on this topic:

> Listening to somebody else's ideas is the one way to know whether the story you believe about the world—as well as about yourself and your place in it—remains intact. We all need to examine our beliefs, air them out and let them breathe. Hearing what other people have to say, especially about concepts we regard as foundational, is like opening a window in our minds and in our hearts. Speaking up is important. Yet to speak up without listening is like banging pots and pans together: Even if it gets your attention, it's not going to get you respect.[106]

Right now, I'm listening to a podcast from a political leader who is sharing his convictions with a group of black hip-hop artists. They are talking about civil rights, reparations, systemic racism, war, and the assassinations of John F. Kennedy and Dr. Martin Luther King Jr. I'm learning and growing as I listen to black Americans discuss these issues.

Listening is the art of great leaders. Abraham Lincoln surrounded himself with leaders who had different views than his. As the

Supreme Commander of the Allied Forces in World War II, General Dwight D. Eisenhower had to navigate the opinions of Winston Churchill, Bernard Montgomery, George Patton, and many other fiery, opinionated, and stubborn leaders. But such men understood that there is wisdom and truth in listening to others.

By listening to other views and perspectives, you might find that you have been wrong about some issues. You might change your mind. But it's important to remember that listening does not necessarily mean adopting. Listening to opposing views will only strengthen your understanding on a given topic. In fact, research has shown that challenging your own views and values makes you "think even harder and produce better arguments to defend [them]."[107]

In short, in developing the habit of being a truth seeker, learn the art of listening to others with whom you disagree. It will make you a richer, more profound, and a more compassionate person!

Building Block 5: Develop a Passion for Reading

I couldn't read well until I was in fifth grade. But I had a teacher, Mrs. Milton, who took me into our elementary school library and told me to find just one short book that interested me and read it from beginning to end. That small habit changed my life. The whole world of great stories was opened to my perspective.

I fell in love with reading biographies and books on history, theology, and leadership. Throughout my high school years, I couldn't wait for classes to end so I could get home and start learning from the books I was reading.

Don't let formal education get in the way of learning! Don't let education get in the way of building a house of truth!

How do we determine when a book is great? It's based on the author. I read authors more than I read individual books; when I find one who speaks to my life, I keep reading more of his or her books. For example, my interest in Winston Churchill was sparked in part through reading *The Last Lion*, the trilogy by William Manchester. As a result, I've read most of Manchester's other historical works. I was turned on to E. Stanley Jones through his writing on the Kingdom of God while I was serving as a missionary in Japan. As a new Christian, I read the classic devotional books of Andrew Murray, E.M. Bounds, Watchman Nee, and R.A. Torrey.

I've read all the books written by Eric Metaxas. I've read almost every historical and biographical work by Doris Kearns Goodwin, David McCullough, and H.W. Brands. In worldview, I've read Francis Schaeffer, Charles Colson, and Jeff Myers. In poetry, Robert Frost is my favorite. In theology, I can't get enough of John Calvin, Martin Luther, George Elton Ladd, Wayne Grudem, and N.T. Wright. In studying the masculine heart, I've read everything John Eldredge has written. On shame and vulnerability, I've read most of the books by Brené Brown.

When you saturate yourself with great authors who write great books about truth, you get equipped in many new areas that bring confidence in times of fear and chaos.

I'm very eclectic, and enjoy many different subjects; you may not be the same. But start somewhere. Start reading. Most great nonfiction authors are truth seekers. Informal reading on subjects that interest you is the avenue to equipping yourself in the journey of becoming the best you in building a house of truth. You are creating your own university.

Ask those you trust which books have deeply influenced them. When you read a book, ask questions like, "How does this line up with my convictions as a Jesus follower?" "Does this author back up what he or she is saying with Scripture and/or source material?" Ask God for His wisdom.

Our culture has overrated formal education and underrated informal learning. I appreciate learning in all its forms, but to be honest, I have learned my greatest lessons and absorbed the most life-changing principles through informal study by reading great authors.

Start reading, start changing. Build a house of truth and become the person God created you to be.

Final Words: Live Not by Lies

All of Western civilization is now living in a post-Christian era, with large numbers of those born after 1970 rejecting the Christian faith. This means that we, as Christians, will face opposition.

A Marxist militancy has rapidly overtaken Western thought. Pope Benedict XVI once described it as a "worldwide dictatorship of seemingly humanistic ideologies"[108] that pushes dissenters to the margins of society. Benedict called this a manifestation of "the spiritual power of the Antichrist."[109] Because they fear truth and desire to "reeducate" us, America's political elite are pushing for censorship of free speech and promoting what we might call "soft totalitarianism."

American Conservative Editor-at-Large Rod Dreher writes, "We cannot hope to resist the coming soft totalitarianism if we do not have our spiritual lives in order."[110] Such was the prophetic voice of the Russian dissident, Nobel laureate, anticommunist activist, and Orthodox Christian Aleksandr Solzhenitsyn whose book *The Gulag Archipelago* exposed the deceit and lies of Russia's Communist leaders. On the eve of his forced exile from his beloved nation, he wrote a final message to the Russian people—an essay titled "Live Not by Lies!"[111]

Solzhenitsyn was not the only dissident who refused to live by lies under a Communist government. Czech playwright and future president Vaclav Havel coined the phrase "live by truth."[112] He realized that under the Communist system, most people had learned to live by lies. He challenged people to rise up and learn the truth.

In the same spirit, we must determine to line our lives up with the truth. To be truth seekers in all areas of life is the habit we must develop to stay strong and courageous.

It takes bravery to build a house of truth. It takes bravery to rest on the Bible as our foundation of truth. It takes bravery to stop letting culture dictate our decisions. It takes bravery to be skeptical of the information we're being fed. It takes bravery to seek out information we disagree with.

But do it. Every day. Do it.

Declaration of Identity (yes, you know the routine; say it ten times):

I am a truth seeker!

Questions to Ponder and Journal

1. Are you building a house of truth in many different disciplines (medical, historical, theological, etc.)? Why or why not?

2. Begin this week to take up the challenge of being a truth seeker by reading, studying, and researching what truth is in many different disciplines. Set aside time each day or week to do the necessary reading.

One way to not have your IQ decrease as you grow older is physical exercise. Your brain uses oxygen, and your brain needs to be clean and well oxygenated. Physical exercise, anaerobic and aerobic, staves off IQ decline over a lifetime.

Dr. Jordan Peterson

I discipline my body like an athlete, training it to do what it should. Otherwise, I fear that after preaching to others I myself might be disqualified.

The Apostle Paul
1 Corinthians 9:27

Habit 8
Work Out Your Problems

I'm taking a break from my busy schedule by spending a few days at our cabin in the Rocky Mountains. A snowstorm passed through last night and the driveway is covered in six inches of snow. First thing this morning, the sun was shining brightly and the forecast called for temperatures rising into the thirties, so I grabbed a snow shovel and got to work.

Our driveway is thirty-five yards long. I started at the garage and began my workout—driving the shovel in and then lifting ten to fifteen pounds of the white stuff. For the next hour I broke a sweat as I gave it all I had. It felt great!

I've learned to love these natural workouts. In this chapter, I am going to challenge you to be brave, strong, and courageous about your mental and physical health.

Habit 8 is "Work out your problems" because if you don't, you will have a lot of them. From deteriorating physical health to brain atrophy, our quality of life will decrease with time.

I am in my sixties, and I have learned that if I don't have good physical and mental health, I don't have anything! Even my brain cells won't be working for me. A noted clinical psychologist has said,

> One way to not have your IQ decrease as you grow older is physical exercise. Your brain uses oxygen, and your brain needs to be clean and well oxygenated. Physical exercise, anaerobic and aerobic, staves off IQ decline over a lifetime.[113]

Realizing the value of continuing to raise my IQ as I grow older, I've been motivated to make a daily workout one of the most important habits of my life. Bethany Hamilton has aptly said, "If you have your health, you have a thousand wishes; if you don't, you have one."

Recent studies in neurology have shown that we can not only maintain our IQ, but we can actually increase our neurological strength even as we grow older. Dr. Alex Dranovsky and Dr. Shawn Achor have written extensively on the fact that we can retrain our minds. Research has shown that the brain can form new neural connections throughout a person's life. This capacity, called neuroplasticity, has wide-ranging implications for everything from intellectual growth to recovering from brain damage.[114]

Neuroscientists are discovering that our brains work like muscles: They get stronger with training. For example, when a person learns a new skill, he creates a new neural pathway. As he develops the skill further, the brain grows and becomes healthier.

The mind is oxygenated best through physical activity, resulting in brain growth. When our brain is well oxygenated, it continues to grow throughout life. You can actually increase your IQ as you grow older through physical exercise!

Physical activity has an immediate impact on your brain that can last for the rest of your life. After years of research, neuroscientist Wendy Suzuki has concluded that "exercise is *the* single most transformative thing that you can do for your brain."[115] In a famous 2017 TEDx talk, she gave three reasons:

> First, through exercise, there is an immediate increase in the neurotransmitters of our brain, like dopamine, serotonin, and adrenaline. Secondly, exercise improves your mood, and lastly, working out improves your reaction time in decision making.[116]

HABIT 8

I Had a Lot of Problems

Recently, I was on a hike with Liz, traversing boulders along the partially frozen Arkansas River in Buena Vista, Colorado. We were laughing and talking. Our conversation turned to my physical and mental state a decade ago. As you've read, I was leading a large and growing church at the time. I also was regularly experiencing headaches, gout, back pain, and depression. I had a lot of problems.

I also struggled with plantar fasciitis in my feet. Between speaking at five services every weekend and some difficult relationships in my life, I was experiencing consistent physical pain. I had gained weight, and to make matters worse, I was battling anxiety and depression on a regular basis. This wasn't just related to lack of exercise, but relational problems between the staff members at the church. The issues were all compounding into a cauldron of ill health.

During that time, I wrote in my journal while on a hunting trip, "I feel so down. I am wondering if this is my last hunt! What's wrong with my life?" That fall I honestly reevaluated the direction of my life. Liz and I began to pray about the future and what kind of changes were needed.

Those changes were incremental and arduous at first. Some days I felt so lethargic I could barely get out of bed. But with God's help, I didn't quit. I read books and sought advice from leading health practitioners. Today, I believe I'm in my best shape since my mid-thirties.

Get Up and Go

All of us battle fatigue and stress in the twenty-first century. In a recent survey, 42 percent of Americans said they struggle just to stay active each day; the greatest barrier to moving more is pain..[117]

> Those with osteoarthritis (OA) have an especially challenging time, as OA negatively affects them an average of four days a week. Fifty-nine percent also

said their OA makes moving and exercising more difficult.[118]

Physicians agree that one of the best ways to shed stress and fatigue is through physical exercise. Stress works as an accelerator—either toward working out or burning out. Unfortunately, most Americans choose to burn out. More than three-quarters of U.S. adults say being in shape and looking good are "very important" to them, yet less than a third actually exercise regularly, and nearly half admit they are not active at all.[119] Recently, Robert F. Kennedy Jr. remarked,

> "We must make good health a priority for all Americans...My uncle [President John F. Kennedy] once said, 'Ask not what your country can do for you, but what can you do for your country.' Well, here's something you can do for your country: Do some exercise. Lose some weight. Get yourself in shape. Build your immune system. Why? Because America has the highest healthcare bills on the planet. We pay $4.3 trillion for healthcare with the worst health outcomes in the world! It is bankrupting us. Eighty percent of that is from chronic disease. We have control over this. Most Americans have bad health habits."[120]

Let's work out our problems with the courage to break through into new health. We can't do difficult things if we are not in good shape. Everything becomes hard if we don't have good oxygen levels, physical strength, and mental calmness. If we are often tired, we get lazy and lethargic; we can't perform at optimal levels, and our brains atrophy. But instead of developing new healthy habits that involve activity, most people turn to pharmaceutical quick fixes that mask the true source of their pain and rarely fix anything.

HABIT 8

I've lived in Colorado Springs, Colorado, for more than thirty years. At seven thousand feet above sea level, it has one of the highest elevations of any city in America. In that time, I have watched dozens of people move from our city to states with lower altitudes because they blamed that for their fatigue and shortness of breath. But it turns out that most of the time, it wasn't the altitude but their *attitude* that was impacting their oxygen levels. They didn't want to exercise, and I'm sad to say, they took their inactivity with them when they moved. Most of them later reported that the move to a lower elevation made little or no difference in their physical problems.

> Studies show that people who regularly and systematically exercise and stay active think better, feel better, and get more done. Both the American College of Sports Medicine and the American Heart Association say Americans should exercise for at least thirty minutes five times a week.[121]

Regardless of your age, sex, or physical ability, exercise can change your life! Researchers at the Mayo Clinic have conducted extensive research into the value of regular physical activity. Here's what they've found:

1. **Exercise controls your weight.** Working out can help prevent excess weight gain or help maintain weight loss. Engaging in physical activity burns calories. The more intense the activity, the more calories you burn.

2. **Exercise combats adverse health conditions and disease.** The Mayo Clinic reports, "Worried about heart disease? Hoping to prevent high blood pressure? No matter what your current weight is, being active boosts high-density lipoprotein (HDL) cholesterol, the "good" cholesterol, and decreases unhealthy triglycerides. This one-two punch keeps your blood flowing smoothly, which decreases your risk of cardiovascular diseases."[122]

3. **Exercise improves mood.** Do you need an emotional lift? Or need a release after a stressful day? Try working out with isometric exercise, lifting weights, or taking a walk. "Physical activity stimulates various brain chemicals that may leave you feeling happier, more relaxed, and less anxious."[123]

4. **Exercise boosts energy.** Exercise delivers oxygen and nutrients to your tissues and helps your cardiovascular system work more efficiently. And when your heart and lung health improve, you have more energy to tackle daily chores.

5. **Exercise promotes better sleep.** Struggling to snooze? Regular physical activity can help you fall asleep faster and deepen your sleep. Just don't exercise too close to bedtime or you may be too energized to go to sleep.

6. **Exercise can be fun...and social.** Exercise and physical activity can be enjoyable. A good workout can give you an opportunity to unwind, enjoy the outdoors, or simply engage in activities that make you happy. Physical activity can also help you connect with family or friends. [124]

Quantity and Quality of Life

God determines the *quantity* of our years, but we determine the *quality* of them. I have always taught Hebrews 12:1 from a spiritual perspective, but as I have grown older and seen the physical toll life takes on many believers, I believe it also has a physical and mental meaning. The passage reads, "Let us run with endurance the race that is set before us..." Physical endurance is necessary for spiritual endurance!

Doesn't it make sense that we have a responsibility to ourselves, our spouses, our children, and our grandchildren to work out and stay physically healthy? The Apostle Paul wrote in 1 Corinthians 9:27,

"I discipline my body like an athlete, training it to do what it should. Otherwise, I fear that after preaching to others I myself might be disqualified." Paul understood how bodily health correlates with spiritual vitality.

I watched my grandparents fade away. My maternal grandfather was a rancher, businessman, and farmer, with my grandmother working by his side. In the prime of their lives, they had been full of energy and physical strength. They built thriving and successful businesses. But I only knew this because of the stories that were handed down. *They never exercised or took care with the food they ate.* The last decade of their lives consisted of one medical emergency and hospital visit after another. They were overweight, tired, and full of ailments in their latter years. As a young man, it was excruciating for me to observe this.

As a pastor, I often counsel folks who have lost all their energy, mental acumen, and love of life. It's especially hard to watch people who once were full of life and joy lose their zest for living due to constant physical issues that could have been avoided.

Five Steps to Transform Your Health

We have the power to change! God has given us the power to transform our lives. But it takes strength and courage to do it. Set your sights on a new you, a better you, an invigorated you. Embrace Habit 8! If you already have an exercise routine, I hope this chapter will only inspire you to continue with zeal. If you are one of the two-thirds of Americans who don't, may I challenge you with some simple ways to better yourself physically and mentally? Here are five incremental steps to working out your problems.

Step 1: A Little Is Better Than None

As someone who competed at the highest levels of my sport through college, for many years I couldn't imagine a weekly exercise routine that was anything short of excruciating. One of the great discoveries in my journey to better mental and physical health is that a little is better than none. In other words, I would rather consistently do a little exercise or a short workout than do nothing.

> *It's liberating not to be overly stressed about the perfect workout routine. Rather, I am now motivated by the vision of consistent activity that I can maintain versus sporadic, hardcore workouts that are done off and on.*

There are many days when I just am not motivated to do a strenuous workout—but I can dig up a little time to go on a short prayer walk, do some air squats, or walk outside on my property and split some wood. The old me would just shrug off both and then feel guilty.

Any personal trainer will tell you that the biggest mistake their clients make is setting goals that are too lofty (i.e., "new year's resolutions") and then quitting a month later because maintaining such a schedule is too difficult. Isn't it better to consistently do a little than starting with too much and then quitting because it's too hard?

I'm not a healthcare or exercise expert, so everything I'm going to advise you on should be checked out by one before you start. But these are some of the "little" workouts I do on a regular basis:

- Knee bends (air squats) next to my desk at work;

- Not asking my assistant to do or get anything I can do or get myself by walking down the hall;

- Taking a ten-minute break to walk around the church campus several times;

- Knocking out a few push-ups when no one's in my office.

Little workouts build confidence, and confidence builds momentum. The small steps of regular workouts began retraining my mind and body toward health when I was at my worst. Today I have a regular routine that involves a mix of weights, walking, and outdoor activities that have had a huge impact on my overall outlook on life.

Let me challenge you to start somewhere and do something different each day that involves staying deliberately active. Here is a simple workout almost anyone can do.

Step 2: The 3x3 Ten-Minute Workout

Adopting a new exercise routine can be daunting. It can be hard to know how to start. I would *not* recommend buying a gym membership, but rather begin with some isometric exercises (bodyweight activities that involve consciously contracting your muscles and holding the squeeze for a set period of time). This can be done anywhere, anytime, with no equipment.

When you need a workout but don't have much time, I would suggest this simple ten-minute routine that can strengthen your core (and even be enjoyable).

1. **Relax.** Find some great music or a podcast. Put on your headphones. Breathe in and out for thirty to sixty seconds and just relax.

2. **Pelvic curls.** Amy Cardin, a Pilates instructor in Providence, Rhode Island, always starts her workouts with pelvic curls. "It's a great way to incorporate some glute and hamstring work into your routine," she says. Begin by lying on your back with your knees bent and your feet on the floor about hip-distance apart. Your arms should be by your sides. Firmly press your lower back into the floor and peel your hips toward the ceiling, creating a bridge with your body. Hold for a few seconds, then, peel your spine back down. Do three sets of three.[125]

3. **Leg lifts.** Next, turn over and get on all fours. Stack your knees under your hips and your hands under your shoulders, then alternate lifting each leg toward the ceiling. Do three sets of three for each leg.

4. **Air squats**. Stand up with your feet shoulder-length apart. Keeping your knees over your feet, squat down as far as you can, then stand back up. Do three sets of three.

5. **Knee push-ups.** Last but not least, try to do a few knee push-ups. Get back down on all fours, knees under your hips and hands under your shoulders, bend your elbows to lower your chest toward the floor, and then press yourself back up. Do three sets of three.

I will make a promise to you. If you do this simple ten-minute workout five times a week, you will have so much more energy that you will get addicted to staying healthy. If you get hooked on a simple, low-impact workout like this one, you may be challenged to go for more.

Step 3: The Sunshine Vitamin

Vitamin D is the sunshine vitamin. Because of my love for the outdoors, I think it's the Happiness Vitamin! You can get all the Vitamin D you need for each new day by getting outside in the sun for thirty minutes. Studies have shown that 88 percent of Americans are deficient in Vitamin D—so that probably includes you. So, listen up.

> *Your body produces Vitamin D naturally when it's directly exposed to sunlight. The National Institutes of Health recommend spending thirty minutes a day outside with no sunscreen or sunglasses to get your daily allowance of Vitamin D. Most of your Vitamin D is absorbed through your eyes.*

I'm not always successful, but I do try to get out several times a week for a brisk walk in the sun. You can also get Vitamin D through certain foods and supplements to maintain adequate levels in your blood.

HABIT 8

What does Vitamin D do for you?

- It promotes calcium absorption in the gut, which helps maintain adequate calcium and phosphate concentrations to strengthen and grow bones.

- It reduces inflammation and optimizes cell growth.

- It strengthens your immune system.

- It reduces depression, gives you more energy, and boosts weight loss. [126]

The benefits of getting into the sunshine would take a whole book to explain (and indeed, many books have been written about just this one vitamin). Let me suggest that getting out in the sun daily for thirty minutes can change your overall health more than you can imagine. Vitamin D can transform your overall demeanor.

Step 4: A 5k Every Day

For almost a decade I've been doing a 5K every day. But I'm not talking about running 3.1 miles. Believe me, I'm no runner! Rather, I want to challenge you to get in five thousand steps each day. I have already shared in Habit 3 about how I learned to walk—really walk. I have now made a weekly and sometimes even daily routine of taking a walk.

Liz and I combine our daily dose of Vitamin D and a good cardio workout through walking together. This is often a time of deep sharing and prayer; other times we walk in silence and just enjoy the scenery. Every day it's different. But a brisk walk has been therapeutic for us.

Many studies show how important walking can be, but let me share my reasons for taking a thirty-minute brisk walk each day.

- It clears my mind.

- It gives me time to think and process.

- It gives me time for prayer.

- It improves my cardiovascular fitness.

- It strengthens my bones and muscle tone.

- I get my daily dosage of Vitamin D.

- It improves my memory.

- It helps me sleep better at night.

- It strengthens my immune system.

- It reduces stress.

I wear a watch that records my steps each day to make sure I get in at least five thousand. You may not feel that's possible right now, but if you start with a goal of getting in a thousand steps per day, you can build from there. The value is worth the effort.

Step 5: Healthy Nutrition

Our bodies are so complex that it's difficult to give advice on nutrition. As I've stated, I'm not an expert. Through research and interviews with experts, I have developed a few principles that drive many of my eating habits. The following five principles come from my daughter-in-law, Chandler Holt, who is a registered nurse and certified in functional medicine. I encourage you to check all this out with a professional nutritional coach and your doctor.

Principle 1: Get Enough Animal-Based Protein

Our bodies require protein to build muscle, collagen, hair, nails, skin, bones, and organ tissue. Without enough protein, our bodies begin to break themselves down to get the protein they need to function, usually resulting in muscle loss. This in turn drives fat gain, which sparks a host of unhealthy cycles. Therefore, focusing on protein is the first principal to getting and maintaining a healthy body.

The human body requires twenty different amino acids to function properly, and nine of them are classified as *essential*. These essential amino acids come only through food. Although you can find them in a variety of foods, they are most easily absorbed by the body through animal sources like eggs, meat, fish, and dairy. A good rule of thumb is ingesting 0.8–1.2 grams of protein per day for each pound of your ideal body weight, with a minimum of eighty to 100 grams a day.

Principle 2: Eliminate Polyunsaturated Fatty Acids

Polyunsaturated fatty acids (PUFAs) are fats that are usually liquid at room temperature. When exposed to oxygen and heat, these fatty acids release free radicals, which are linked to cancers, accelerated aging, and autoimmune disease. PUFAs are found in sunflower, canola, flax seed, corn, safflower, and other nut or seed oils that we often cook with. Begin to replace these oils with grass-fed butter, coconut oil, tallow, or ghee.

Principle 3: Focus on Minerals

Potassium, sodium, and magnesium (among many other minerals) are needed for many key bodily functions. Due to America's modern farming practices and poor water quality, unfortunately our food is now very low in the minerals a healthy body needs. Focusing on mineral-rich foods like fruits, organ meats, and beverages like coconut water and hibiscus tea, as well as supplementing your diet with mineral drops in your water, can be very helpful in making sure your body runs at optimal levels.

Principle 4: Prioritize Simple over Complex Carbs

The Glycemic Index (GI) ranks foods on a scale of 0–100 by how quickly they raise your blood sugar levels (100 being the worst for you). Eating simple carbs like fruit, fresh fruit juice, high-quality dairy, root vegetables, and well-cooked leafy greens is much better for you than more complex carbs like rice or bread.

A common misconception is that fruit and fruit juices are not good because "they are high in sugar." But a glass of fresh orange juice has a GI of only 48, whereas a piece of store-bought bread has a GI of around 100.

Principle 5: Balance Blood Sugar

Something we hear little about is how to balance one's blood sugar. But one simple way to do this is to pair every protein with a carbohydrate.

When we consume protein, our body calls for the hormone insulin to be released in order to move that protein into our cells. But when protein isn't paired with carbs, our bodies don't have anything to keep our blood sugar levels stable, and therefore our blood sugar drops. Good protein/carb pairings include eating fruit with cheese, drinking a glass of orange juice alongside a plate of scrambled eggs, or having a steak with a side of sauteed zucchini.

Take Control of Your Life!

This chapter might seem daunting to some of you. Ten years ago it would have been overwhelming to me! But I realized that continuing to do the same things I had been doing wasn't working. I had to develop some new habits, so I did. It's made a big difference in how I feel. I started with small changes and increased my knowledge and discipline gradually.

Now my mind and body are stronger than ever, and I'm pumped to keep getting stronger, smarter, and more peaceful in my mind, body, and spirit even as I age. How about you?

HABIT 8

Declaration of Identity (shout it out ten times):

I am getting mentally and physically healthier day by day!

Questions to Ponder and Journal

1. Will you set up a time each day to do the 3x3 ten-minute workout? Get advice from your doctor, and then set it up in your schedule.

2. Will you try to do your workout at least three to four times per week? Identify any obstacles that might prevent you from doing this, and write down how you plan to eliminate them. What alternate plan can you execute when "life" gets in the way?

3. What routine can you maintain consistently? You already know the answer.

*Because so many have asked me what I do in my personal workout, I have included it here. My caveat to those who haven't worked out much is to get a Physical and advice from a healthcare professional before attempting the following:

Thirty -minute walk. (If I can't do this, I use an elliptical machine.) One set of thirty push-ups, one set of thirty air squats, one set of ten curls with twenty-pound dumbbells. I do this circuit five times with a one- to two-minute break between sets.

We are half-hearted creatures, fooling about with drink and sex and ambition when infinite joy is offered us, like an ignorant child who wants to go on making mud pies in a slum because he cannot imagine what is meant by the offer of a holiday at the sea. We are far too easily pleased.

C.S. Lewis

"The first of all the commandments is: ... And you shall love the Lord your God with all your heart, with all your soul, with all your mind, and with all your strength ... And the second, like it, is this: 'You shall love your neighbor as yourself.' There is no other commandment greater than these."

Jesus

Mark 12:28–31

Habit 9
Be Wholehearted

Every fall in Colorado, the Worshipper Warrior Men's Ministry leads a "Wholeheart Advance" with men from around the nation. This is a challenging four-day conference on wholehearted living. Each message is designed to target some aspect of the masculine heart. In seven-person groups of "bloodstained allies," the men open their hidden places of shame, failure, and those unmentionables that no one wants to talk about. We get real and open about the dark places of our hearts. We challenge the men to leave their half-hearted existence and take the risk of wholehearted living through intimacy with God and other men. We go deep—and we see miracles happen.

Whenever I walk onto the stage, I am greeted by this challenge and response: "Whole heart—live free!" We shout this with gusto three times. Upon hearing this shout for the first time, one new participant said, "I haven't heard such shouting from men since my college football days!"

On the first day, few understand what they're saying, but as the conference progresses, the mantra takes on new meaning.

God cares more about our hearts than anything else. The Bible has more to say about the heart than any other topic—24,232 of the Bible's 31,102 verses mention or allude to it. That means 77 percent of the Bible deals with the heart!

Being wholehearted is the theme of the Kingdom of God! This is the way into freedom. Living with a free heart under the power of the Holy Spirit is the source of our creativity, joy, courage, and strength. We've been put on this earth to live wholeheartedly.

Breakthrough Courage

As I conclude this book, it seems fitting to close with this one habit that encapsulates all of them. If we miss this habit, we will never become the courageous men and women that God created us to be. Being wholehearted is the fuel for all the rest. It's in the combination of wholehearted living that we are empowered to keep fighting and not give in to the fears and anxiety that have plagued our lives.

Wholehearted living is your God-created nature in action—not just a concept, but an action that becomes a habit. Awakening each day with the spiritual, emotional, and mental conviction to live with authenticity in our marriage, family, job, and relationships is the core of living from the heart.

Live Free

Iranaeus, one of the early church fathers, must have been thinking about wholeheartedness when he wrote, "The glory of God is a man fully alive."[127] Wholeheartedness is living as God's image: alive and fully engaged with our heart, soul, mind, and strength in every facet of life. It's the sum of who we are. It's lining up our lives under the rubric of the Kingdom of God. Jesus was speaking of the wholehearted life when He said,

> "The first of all the commandments is… you shall love the Lord your God with all your heart, with all your soul, with all your mind, and with all your strength." (Mark 12:28–30)

This is truly the wholehearted life of freedom—the freedom to love with our entire being. It's about belonging to Christ, worshipping Him, and finding intimate connection with the Holy Spirit. It's loving God with the passion and power of God and breaking out of the spirit of fear. Wholehearted living is the summation of all the other habits coming together into the wonderful freedom of authenticity.

Loving from our heart, soul, mind, and strength is the true self that we have always longed for. It's why we watch the movies and read the stories of people who have given their hearts and lives to a cause or a conviction. It's how we define the word "heroic." When we see men and women risking all to rescue someone, we are touched deeply because the theme resonates with something deep in our soul.

In the movie *The Guardian*, Coast Guard veteran Ben Randall (played by Kevin Costner) trains young men for service. He develops a close relationship with the cocky but talented rookie, Jake Fischer (played by Ashton Kutcher). In the final scene, Ben and Jake are being pulled up from the sea into the helicopter after a rescue when the steel cord holding them begins to unravel. From his many years of experience, it's clear to Ben that it will not hold them both. With Jake protesting, Ben cuts himself loose, falling back into the stormy sea so that Jake might live. This is the kind of love that deeply inspires us because it's the way of Kingdom of God. Jesus said, "Greater love has no one than this, than to lay down his life for his friends" (John 15:13).

The life lived in wholehearted devotion involves connecting with people and loving them as an overflow of our experience with the love of God. Jesus continues,

> *"And the second [commandment], like it, is this: 'You shall love your neighbor as yourself.' There is no other commandment greater than these."* (Mark 12:31)

The true freedom of the Jesus follower leads to loving ourselves and other people. These are two sides of the same spiritual coin. Loving God and loving ourselves means we realize our value and identity before God and those around us. The struggle we all have is knowing ourselves and our mistakes. But this is the line of demarcation between the half-hearted and the wholehearted: Both see the failures, shame, and brokenness of their lives, but the wholehearted choose to press into the shame for the greater goal of liberty.

The half-hearted cannot face the pain of their own mistakes and brokenness. Fear grips their hearts. But wholehearted people face the pain, the shame, and the failures because they know they are worthy of love and in Christ, they are enough. They have nothing to hide.

Realizing our value as a child of God leads us into love for others. Love leads to intimacy with people—and intimacy is not easy, especially with people we don't like. Loving those who are unloving is an integral part of loving God with our whole heart. This is hard work, but it's worth pursuing. It's worth going after with all our being. Living and loving in the freedom of God's power is the wholehearted life.

Barriers to Freedom

But such freedom comes with a price. One can't walk in freedom without being honest about the barriers. Wholehearted living is about engaging the impediments to that freedom. Wholehearted living takes courage. It means we take on the bad stuff, the dark shame caves, and our selfishness. It takes discipline to be fully alive.

It's learning to be honest and accept ourselves as valuable, loved, and important. It's the value we place on God, ourselves, and the people we consider bloodstained allies (Habit 3). It is believing by faith that we are created in the image of God, fully blessed with gifts, talents, and skills that He wants to use.

Being wholehearted is accepting ourselves and believing God has made us for belonging and connection.

This is what we mean by "whole heart…live free." Truly living out the "wholeheart advance" of our personhood will always lead to freedom. Jesus wants each of us walking in the DNA of the Kingdom of God: righteousness, peace, and joy (Habit 1). But there is an enemy who hates you and wants to keep you in bondage.

One of the parts of my job as a church planter and pastor that I absolutely love is developing people, specifically other leaders. This is the greatest joy of my life. Our mission statement at The Road is "Empowering People to Change the World." I take that mission seriously. We want each leader to walk in his or her full potential in Christ through wholehearted living.

In developing wholehearted people into leaders, we are honest about our faults and defects. We have had to wrestle with impediments and walls that block us from living out our true God-given natures. It's hard work and to be frank, often unsettling. No one enjoys being vulnerable about their sin.

The false self, the fake self, hinders the emergence of the truly wholehearted self, the image-of-God self. This barrier, more than anything else, blocks the heart of the individual from experiencing the power of God. We have grown accustomed to accepting our false self because it's familiar and has never been challenged.

Most Christians have learned the culture of Christianity and thus, know how to act and what to say to please people—but they don't know how to be authentic. Basically, we become fakers in our outward appearance in order to protect our places of pain (which isn't our true self, we just think it is). We cover up who we truly are, promoting self-deception and sabotaging wholehearted living in the process.

False Self: Poser

Satan doesn't want us to experience the freedom of the wholehearted life; he will do anything to keep us shackled to a false version of ourselves, tightly twisted within the chains of oppression. This is the false self, the pseudo self. Jesus told us Satan's job description: "The thief does not come except to steal, and to kill, and to destroy" (John 10:10a).

Satan and his demons come *only* to steal away your heart, kill your desires, and destroy your identity! The great satanic lie is that your value is based only on your outward achievements, accolades, and appearance. This deception creates a false version of you. It builds a distorted perspective of who you are and why you're on this earth.

Satan's devices create within us the desire to play hide-and-seek with God, ourselves, and others. We learn to be pretenders and posers. We develop a habit of running from any truth that makes us feel uncomfortable or vulnerable. We hide behind the veneer of success and impenetrable confidence. We echo in our heart statements like: "I am a rock; I am independent; I don't need anyone."

As posers, we cover up our shame and humiliation. We learn to embellish and exaggerate our "exploits" to be accepted and honored. It's just too uncomfortable to live any other way. Most of us don't have an environment that enables us to live any other way. I see it all the time—even in our church. When people approach me as the senior pastor, they start doing the religious posing they learned in other churches. For them, everything revolves around their positive points and their accomplishments.

We think life consists of the pecking order of the cool and uncool. We learn it in grade school and become experts on it as the years go by. To be in the cool crowd, we memorize the playbook and talk, act, and maneuver accordingly.

Posers live in the fear of somehow being found out. We practice what we preach to ourselves: "I will never be found out. I will never open up. People will hurt me if I'm truly honest about my stuff." We don't want to be known because we fear what would happen if our shame, defeats, and deficiencies were exposed. Thus, we live a life of half-truths, innuendos, and counterfeits.

Half-Hearted Pleasure

We have become convinced that life is only about pleasure, so we restrict our existence to the pursuit of our next gratification. We sell our souls to drink, sex, and ambition. But our heart is only half engaged! Our heart is anything but alive. In *The Weight of Glory*, C.S. Lewis, the great Oxford professor, writes,

> If there lurks in most modern minds the notion that to desire our own good and earnestly to hope for the enjoyment of it is a bad thing, I submit that this notion has crept in from Kant and the Stoics and is no part of the Christian faith. Indeed, if we consider the unblushing promises of reward and the staggering nature of the rewards promised in the Gospels, it would seem that our Lord finds our desires not too strong, but too weak. We are half-hearted creatures, fooling about with drink and sex and ambition when infinite joy is offered us, like an ignorant child who wants to go on making mud pies in a slum because he cannot imagine what is meant by the offer of a holiday at the sea. We are far too easily pleased.[128]

Some of us have grown up in Christian traditions that downplay emotions and passion. Influenced strongly by monasticism or stoic philosophies, such churches have knowingly or unknowingly suggested that real spirituality is subdued and controlled. Strong emotions are bad, they say, and living with passion is dangerous.

Lewis makes an interesting point—the opposite of stoicism. He is saying that embracing strong desires creates the atmosphere for wholehearted living! Lewis is challenging us to pursue the "staggering nature of the rewards promised in the Gospels" with robust passion. He even says that it is the *half-hearted* who are fooling around with drink, sex, and ambition. *What is needed is not less passion but more passion, rightly directed.* To be fully alive and wholehearted is to be in touch with our sanctified emotions with all our heart, soul, mind, and strength, focused on Christ. We are called to the wholehearted pursuit of joy.

Jesus is challenging us to fully love God with all our heart, with all our soul, with all our mind, and with all our strength because this is the way to being fully alive! This brings all of life fully together within the homeland of the soul. This is the rubric of the Kingdom of God. This is the wild adventure of wholehearted living.

The Wild Adventure

As an outdoorsman, I have often camped in the wilderness. At night, the seemingly tame forest becomes altogether different; it becomes wild. In the darkness, you hear savage sounds—the screech of a wounded rabbit, the hoot of an owl, the howl of coyotes, and the bugle of elk. It's anything but tame. God made all living things wild because He loves wildness.

A wild God isn't a concept most of us are comfortable with. In our civilized, organized, and comfortable Western Christianity, we've been taught to embrace a tame, predictable God of our own making. In The *Chronicles of Narnia*, C.S. Lewis paints a picture of God as Aslan, a lion.

> (Mrs. Beaver says) "If there's anyone who can appear before Aslan without their knees knocking, they're either braver than most or else just silly."
> "Then is he safe?" said Lucy.
> "Safe?" said Mr. Beaver. "Don't you hear what Mrs. Beaver tells you? Who said anything about safe? Course he isn't safe. But he's good. He's the King, I tell you."[129]

God is not tame; He is wild and out of our control. He also hasn't created you and me to be tame and in control. We were not created for the tameness of safety and predictability. We were not originally formed for hiddenness and concealment.

God created us for the wildness of being our true selves. Adam and Eve were "both naked but they were not ashamed" (Genesis

2:24b). They were, in their original state, fully exposed to God and each other. Shame had no power over them; they did not even know it. They were given a wild garden in which to "rule over every living thing...to be fruitful and multiply" (Genesis 1–2). *They were wildly free.*

Jesus called it the "abundant life" (John 10:10b). We were created to experience fully alive hearts and to immerse it in love, belonging, and connection. Proverbs 4:23 says, "Keep your heart with all diligence, for out of it *spring* (my italics) the issues of life." It is from the heart that our deepest passions and desires flow.

From the heart springs our longing for adventure. This is the wild, true self. This is what God created you to experience.

You were born again for the wild adventure of discovering your true self as a child of God. The true self is a heart fully given over to the wild God of abundance. Only God knows how to lead you and guide you into this adventure. The fruitful life is the adventure of love, belonging, and connection. It is in loving God, belonging to His family, and connecting with people that we come alive into wholehearted passion.

The epic adventure of our lives is to tackle our heart with all its shortcomings, sinful ways, and broken promises. It's about failing, getting rejected, and yet continuing to show up. If you continually show up, the adventure of wholehearted living will grow and mature within you over time.

What if this wildness of heart is actually the life that should be "ordinary"? In living in a monastery year after year, Thomas Merton discovered that the ordinary life was becoming fully alive as a man by becoming the person God created him to be—one not distorted by greed, ambition, or lust.

We need to have greater passion for holy, wild, wholehearted living than we do for unholy, lustful living. The choice is ours. To give oneself to the wholehearted life is to have a greater passion for the abundant life than for our fleshly desires. How many sermons have you heard admonishing you to wildly holy living? Not too many.

But I would venture to say that if the world could see men and women who call themselves Jesus followers living with the wild adventure of wholehearted zeal, we could upset this world like the early disciples did. Those early believers in Christ were described as people who "turned the world upside down" (Acts 17:6). I believe that if you can begin to develop the habits contained in this book, you will shake up the world around you.

Such wholehearted passion flows out of knowing that we are deeply loved.

Beloved and Worthy

When Jesus was baptized, the Father said, "This is My beloved Son, in whom I am well pleased" (Matthew 3:17). Before Jesus had done anything outwardly—before He had healed anyone, preached to anyone, or cast out one demon—the Father said of Him, "This is My beloved Son." In the same manner, the Father says to each of us, "You are created in My image; you are My beloved child. I created you to be wholehearted." Brennan Manning challenges us to define ourselves

> Radically as one beloved by God. God's love for you and his choice of you constitute your worth. Accept that, and let it become the most important thing in your life.[130]

The ordinary self is the beloved self. The poser needs attention for achievements and the adulation of others. The true self is wild, adventurous, and beloved. Manning continues, "Our true self needs neither a muted trumpet to herald our arrival nor a gaudy soapbox to rivet attention from others."[131] Knowing we are beloved is the anthem of the wholehearted. It is a free spirit that knows we belong.

We are worthy of belonging. One author writes, "If we want to fully experience love and belonging, we must believe that we are worthy of love and belonging."[132] We let go of what people say about us, own our stories—by embracing our belovedness and worthiness—and accept that we are enough in God's sight. Though those around us may not always see us this way, we learn to put more faith in God's promises than the opinions of others.

It's in the authentic environment of living our story that we discover the wholehearted life of belonging and love. It is believing that we are worthy and beloved right now—not tomorrow and not when we "get our act together," but today, in the present.

Having the faith to believe that we are beloved and that we belong does not require us to change to fit in. Rather, it requires that we be who we are. It's the natural way; it's the Kingdom of God way—the ordinary way that we have longed for since birth. We *are* beloved. We *do* belong. We are "in Christ." This is the wholehearted, honest, true life we were created to live.

A Journey

The habit of wholehearted living is a lifelong journey. Since it's grounded in how we handle relationships, setbacks are inevitable. Incremental in its growth, it's literally two steps forward and one step back, daily. It's a choice we make every day to be real, to be authentic, to be loving. It's trying, getting knocked down, being embarrassed, and yet choosing to get up again. It's more like a boxing match than summiting a peak.

There's no answer sheet for this test. The relational nature of authentic living is unpredictable and indefinable. Connection is about traversing the unknown space between people. Our responsibility is not the outcome, but the journey. We do our best at the time to love as Jesus would love—with wholehearted affection—but we have no guarantees that this love will be reciprocated.

We are going to take some nasty punches. We will be rejected. We will be mistreated. But wholehearted people get back up, go back to the corner, and show up again the next day. We may be knocked down, but we are never knocked out.

We bandage our wounds and step back into the ring—or to use Roosevelt's vernacular, we step back into the arena. The arena is full of malevolent people who want to hurt you. But the strength and courage to get back in there is the stuff of wholehearted living. Churchill once said,

> Courage is rightly esteemed the first of human qualities...because it is the quality which guarantees all others.[133]

The courage to get back up after getting knocked down is the quality that guarantees wholehearted living. It is the deep-seated conviction that real joy is found in the journey. One might say that to be strong and courageous *is* the journey.

Remember when I mentioned the road less traveled? Well, this is it—the ultimate journey into the unknown of vulnerability and authenticity. Wholehearted living means we keep trying to find our center in Christ, sharing our heart with bloodstained allies, and when we fail, we get right back up and try again. The destination is the process. It is living wholeheartedly the crucified life:

> *I have been crucified with Christ; it is no longer I who live, but Christ lives in me; and the life which I now live in the flesh I live by faith in the Son of God, who loved me and gave Himself for me.* (Galatians 2:20)

We get back up on the cross each day. This means allowing Christ to live His life through us. Belonging, belovedness, and love are not just things we give or get; they are part of our growth into maturity.

Liz and I have been married for nearly forty years, and we are still learning the art of wholehearted living. It's a "together" project that unifies us through the risk of wildly loving God and each other. We still get upset at each other at times, and we must continually practice crucifying ourselves in order to love the other. But it's worth it.

Since I launched out in attempting to live the wholehearted life, I've had ebbs and flows. From the inception around the fire pit with a few trustworthy men, to the boatload of challenges through the years, I wouldn't trade for anything the new me that is emerging. The pain of the battle has been worth the authenticity I've gained.

You are called to the wholehearted life! It is your destiny. God's wild adventure awaits your willingness to enter life with the wholehearted conviction that, despite your imperfections, failures, and shame, you belong. God loves you and He says that you are beloved.

Enter the arena.

Declaration of Identity (shout it out ten times):

I am a wholehearted person! I am beloved and I belong!

Questions to Ponder and Journal

1. How would you define "wholehearted living"?

2. Why is wholehearted living the culmination of all the other habits?

3. How are you going to live your life differently as a result of reading this book?

Final Thoughts: Choose Dangerous

I come alive in the wild. Woods, streams, and mountain vistas bring joy to my heart. I find joy in such settings because the wild adventure of following Christ is prophetically reflected through the wildness of nature. I'm penning these words while seated in a grove of aspen trees at ten thousand feet in the Rocky Mountains. A mule deer has just walked within twenty-five feet of me, never noticing my presence.

Off in the distance, I can see the Buffalo Peaks Mountain Range. Dark, ominous clouds are obscuring the tops of the snow-covered mountains. The sky over my perch is sunny and cloudless, but as those of us raised in the South say, "a storm is a-brewin'." Soon, I will be enveloped in rain, hail, and snow. The tempest is coming.

Life is dangerous and unpredictable. Maybe you're experiencing a tempest in your life right now. It could be that you are in the center of a relational, marital, or business cyclone. It feels dangerous and you're frightened.

But you no longer need to be buffeted by fear. You don't have to succumb to the narrative of our culture. My hope and prayer are that you will put each of these nine habits into practice and experience breakthrough from fear to courage.

Living the nine habits is about making the Kingdom of God your highest priority, being true to your unique self, and learning to be authentic. Learning to be vulnerable with some bloodstained allies, staying in good physical condition, and facing your shame and failure is not easy stuff, but it's so worth it. You can quit being a poser and live out of a dangerous new heart; this is the reality you can now embrace.

Embrace the cyclone of fear, failure, and shame. Live the nine habits. Choose to be dangerous. Being strong and courageous is risky business. It wouldn't be an adventure if it wasn't dangerous. In the fourteenth century, the word "adventure" meant "hazardous." To venture out, to take a risk, is inherently hazardous. We live in dangerous times for dangerous people.

I want to challenge you to live dangerously. Dangerous people are those who live as though they have nothing to lose. And when you begin to seek first the Kingdom of God, making it your passion and priority, all else will pale in comparison. The dangers of the Kingdom are the safest place for the Christian to be.

Live in defiance of this world and take up your cross with love, kindness, passion, and authenticity. Be brave. Be dangerous!

Notes

Introduction

[1] LinkedIn News, "Brené Brown: What's the Difference Between Fear and 'Armor'?", YouTube, February 6, 2019, https://www.youtube.com/watch?v=7LbI19ZiMlI.
[2] "Nearly Two-Thirds of Young Americans Are Fearful About the Future of Democracy in America, Harvard Youth Poll Finds," Harvard Kennedy School of Politics, https://iop.harvard.edu/news/nearly-two-thirds-young-americans-fearful-about-future-democracy-america-harvard-youth-poll.
[3] "Americans Anticipate Higher Stress at the Start of 2023 and Grade Their Mental Health Worse," American Psychiatric Association, December 21, 2022, https://www.psychiatry.org/news-room/news-releases/americans-anticipate-higher-stress-at-the-start-of.
[4] Harvard Kennedy School of Politics. https://iop.harvard.edu/news/nearly-two-thirds-young-americans-fearful-about-future-democracy-america-harvard-youth-poll
[5] American Psychiatric Association. https://www.psychiatry.org/news-room/news-releases/annual-anxiety-and-mental-health-poll-2023
[6] Justin Whitmel Early, *The Common Rule: Habits of Purpose for an Age of Distraction* (Lisle, Illinois: IVP Books, 2023), 7.
[7] Ibid.
[8] James Clear, *Atomic Habits: An Easy and Proven Way to Build Good Habits and Break Bad Ones* (New York: Avery Publishing, 2018), page 65.
[9] David Maraniss, *When Pride Still Mattered: A Life of Vince Lombardi* (New York: Simon & Schuster, 1997), 365.
[10] *The Common Rule*, page 8.
[11] Rosa Cherneva, "The Power of Saying Things Out Loud," Medium, July 13, 2020, https://medium.com/illumination/the-power-of-saying-things-out-loud-c82daa49330a.

Habit 1: Seek the First Thing First

[12] "Major Depression," National Institute of Mental Health, last updated July 2023, https://www.nimh.nih.gov/health/statistics/major-depression.
[13] Jamie Ducharme, "U.S. Suicide Rates Are the Highest They've Been Since

World War II," TIME, June 20, 2019, https://time.com/5609124/us-suicide-rate-increase.

[14] "Johann Wolfgang von Goethe Quotes," Brainyquotes, https://www.brainyquote.com/authors/johann-wolfgang-von-goeth-quotes.

[15] The Young Remnant, "But Seek Ye First the Kingdom of God, and His Righteousness -Jordan Peterson," YouTube, June 26, 2020, https://www.youtube.com/watch?v=Y_-6gqdJbnc.

[16] E. Stanley Jones, *The Unshakable Kingdom and the Unchanging Person* (CreateSpace Independent Publishing Platform, 2017) 47.

[17] Fares Ksebati, "How to Dive Off the Blocks FASTER | Swimming Smart Tips," YouTube, October 15, 2021, https://www.youtube.com/watch?v=9QrKpWnVCZ4.

[18] George Elton Ladd, *The Gospel of the Kingdom* (Chicago: Eerdmans Publishing Company, 1959), 15.

[19] Ibid.

[20] Ibid.

[21] Ibid, 19.

[22] Jones and Bartlett Learning. PDF. Chapter 2: DNA is the Instruction Book for Life.

[23] Ibid.

[24] E. Stanley Jones, *Abundant Living: 364 Daily Devotions* (Nashville: Abingdon Press, 2014), 16.

[25] Ibid,23.

[26] Jeanne Guyon, *Experiencing the Depths of Jesus Christ: Library of Spiritual Classics, Vol. 2* (Jacksonville, Florida:Christian Books Publishing House, 1981), 17.

[27] "Mahatma Gandhi Says he Believes In,Christ But Not Christianity," *The Harvard Crimson*, January 11, 1927, https://www.thecrimson.com/article/1927/1/11/mahatma-gandhi-says-he-believes-in/.

[28] Joseph Whelan, S.J., "Fall in Love," IgnatianSpirituality.com, https://www.ignatianspirituality.com/ignatian-prayer/prayers-by-st-ignatius-and-others/fall-in-love.

[29] *Abundant Living*, 7.

Habit 2: Embrace Hard

[30] Scott Kujak, "85: The Happy Body and Olympic Weightlifting with Jerzy Gregorak," Underdog Scott Kujak, July 14, 2020, https://scottkujak.com/the-happy-body-and-olympic-weightlifting-with-jerzy-gregorek.

[31] Ibid.

[32] The Happy Body, https://thehappybody.com/about-the-creators-jerzy-gregorek-aniela-gregorek.

[33] "Harry Emerson Fosdick Quotes," Brainy Quotes. https://www.brainyquote.com/quotes/harry_emerson_fosdick_154684#:~:text=Harry%20Emerson%20Fosdick%20Quotes&text=He%20who%20knows%20no%20hardships%20will%20know%20no%20hardihood.,a%20strong%20mixture%20of%20troubles.

[34] Nancy Pearcey, *The Toxic War on Masculinity: How Christianity Reconciles the Sexes* (Grand Rapids, Michigan:Baker Books, 2023), 28.

[35] "How Working Improves your Mental Health," Mass General Brigham McLean, October 26, 2023, https://www.mcleanhospital.org/essential/how-working-improves-your-mental-health.

[36] Sonakshi Kohli, "Do You Find Yourself Sitting Idle Often? Here's How It Can Wreck Your Mental Health," HealthShots, last updated May 11, 2021, https://www.healthshots.com/mind/mental-health/do-you-find-yourself-sitting-idle-often-heres-how-it-can-wreck-your-mental-health.

[37] "Rosa Parks: Tired of Giving In," Smithsonian Institute National Portrait Gallery, December 1, 2016, https://npg.si.edu/blog/tired-giving.

[38] Jade Eckardt, "Bethany Hamilton Reflects on Losing Arm to Tiger Shark 20 Years Later," *Surfer*, https://www.surfer.com/trending-news/bethany-hamilton-tiger-shark-20-years.

[39] Blackpast, "(1857): Frederick Douglass: 'If There Is No Struggle, There Is No Progress,'" Blackpast, January 25, 2007, https://www.blackpast.org/african-american-history/1857-frederick-douglass-if-there-no-struggle-there-no-progress.

[40] Quoted in Brené Brown, *Atlas of the Heart: Mapping Meaningful Connection and the Language of Human Experience* (New York: Random House, 2021), 18.

[41] Ibid,20.

[42] Nick Vujicic, "No Arms, no Legs, no Worries" YouTube, September 2, 2017.

[43] Ted, "Grit: The Power of Passion and Perseverance | Angela Lee Duckworth," YouTube, May 9, 2013, https://www.youtube.com/watch?v=H14bBuluwB8.

[44] Ibid.

[45] How Happiness Affects your Success: Interview with Sean Achor. Quoted from Tedx Bloomington, YouTube. https://www.speakersoffice.com/happiness-affects-success-interview-shawn-achor/#:~:text="90%25%20of%20our%20long%2D,we%20can%20then%20affect%20reality."

Habit 3: Develop Bloodstained Allies

[46] Eugene Peterson, *Leap Over a Wall* (New York: HarperCollins, 1997), 53.

[47] G.K. Chesterton, "War and Politics," The Society of G.K. Chesterton, https://www.chesterton.org/quotations/war-and-politics.

[48] The Lonely Islands. Quoted from ThinkTank-inc.org. October 28, 2016.

[49] "U.S. Suicide Rates Are the Highest They've Been Since World War II."

[50] La Leche League International. https://llli.org/news/what-your-baby-knows-about-breastfeeding/

[51] *Gladiator*, directed by Ridley Scott, (Dreamworks Pictures, 2000), 1:24:05, 2:34, https://www.amazon.com/gp/video/detail/B08VTFPQ9Y/ref=atv_dp_sign_su c_3P.

[52] Steve Holt, *Worshipper and Warrior: A 21-Day Journey into the Dangerous Life of David* (Worshipper Warrior Press: Colorado Springs, 2018), 95.

[53] Cited by Michelle Gielan and Shawn Achor, "We're Better Together," Live Happy, January 22, 2018, https://www.shawnachor.com/project/live-happy-better-together.

[54] Shawn Achor, *Big Potential* (New York: Currency, 2018), 76.

[55] Helen Walters, "Vulnerability Is the Birthplace of Innovation, Creativitiy, and Change: Brené Brown at TED 2012," TEDBlog, March 2, 2012, https://blog.ted.com/vulnerability-is-the-birthplace-of-innovation-creativity-and-change-brene-brown-at-ted2012/

Habit 4: Face the Unmentionables

[56] Kathleen Dalton, Theodore Roosevelt: A Strenuous Life (New York: Alfred P. Knopf, 2002), 359.

[57] Brené Brown, *Dare to Lead* (New York: Random House, 2018), 45.

[58] Brené Brown, *The Gifts of Imperfection: Let Go of Who You Think You're Supposed to Be and Embrace Who you Are.* (Center City, Minnesota: Hazelden Publishing, 2010), 65.

[59] Robert Frost, "The Road Not Taken," *Mountain Interval* (New York: Henry Holt and Company, 1916), 9, https://www.gutenberg.org/files/29345/29345-h/29345-h.htm.

[60] Brené Brown, Ibid, 38.

[61] Ibid.

Habit 5: Eat the Book

[62] Eugene Peterson, *Eat the Book* (London: Hodder and Stoughton, 2006), 65.

[63] Evelyn Underhill, *Great Devotional Classics: Selections from Evelyn Underhill* (Nashville:The Upper Room, 1961), 10.

[64] Blair Justice, *Who Gets Sick: Thinking and Health* (Houston: Peak Press, 1987), 126.

[65] *Abundant Living*, 79.

[66] Andy Fell "Mindfulness from Meditation Associated with Lower Stress Hormone," UCDavis, March 27, 2013, https://www.ucdavis.edu/news/mindfulness-meditation-associated-lower-stress-hormone.

[67] Daphne M. Davis and Jeffrey A. Hayes, "What Are the Benefits of Mindfulness," *Monitor on Psychology*, July/August 2012, Vol. 43, No. 7, , https://www.apa.org/monitor/2012/07-08/ce-corner.

[68] Ibid.

[69] William Thornton Whitsett, *My Quiet Hours, Saber and Song* (Whitsett Institute, 1917), 87.

[70] *Experiencing the Depths of Jesus Christ*, 14.

[71] Jan Johnson, *When the Soul Listens: Finding Rest and Direction in Contemplative Prayer* (Amazon Books, 1999), 36.

[72] Henri Nouen, *The Way of the Heart: Connecting with God through Prayer, Wisdom, and Silence* (Morristown, New Jersey: Ballantine Books, 1986), 30.

[73] *Experiencing the Depths of Jesus Christ*, 70.

[74] Ibid, 10.

Habit 6: Practice Gratitude

[75] "Giving Thanks Can Make You Happier," Harvard Health Publishing, August 14, 2021, https://www.health.harvard.edu/healthbeat/giving-thanks-can-make-you-happier#:~:text=In%20positive%20psychology%20research%2C%20gratitude,adversity%2C%20and%20build%20strong%20relationships.

[76] Joel Salatin, *The Marvelous Pigness of Pigs* (Murray, Kentucky: Faith Words, 2016), 84.

[77] *The Gifts of Imperfection*, 98.

[78] Shawn Achor, *The Happiness Advantage* (Surry Hills, New South Wales: Crown Publishing Group, 2010), 34.

[79] Ibid, 98.

[80] Ibid.

[81] "The Happiness Advantage at Work: Begin with Being Grateful," Blue

Beyond Consulting, https://www.bluebeyondconsulting.com/thought-leadership/happiness-advantage-work-begin-grateful.
[82] Ibid.
[83] *New York Times*, https://www.nytimes.com/2020/10/11/business/family-dinner-returns.html. This
[84] *Who Gets Sick*, 257.
[85] Ibid.
[86] Ibid, 261.
[87] Ibid, 263.
[88] Ibid, 264.

Habit 7: Build a House of Truth

[89] Brandon Clay, "What Is Truth? A Christian Perspective," Truth Story, July 8, 2018, https://truthstory.org/blog/what-is-truth.
[90] "Truth," Stanford Encyclopedia of Philosophy, https://plato.stanford.edu/entries/truth/#TarTheTruth, last updated August 16, 2018.
[91] "Johann Sebastian Bach: The Fifth Evangelist," *Christianity Today*, https://www.christianitytoday.com/history/people/musiciansartistsandwriters/johann-sebastian-bach.html.
[92] Abraham Lincoln, "Reply to Loyal Colored People Upon Presentation of a Bible," September 7, 1864, *Collected Works of Abraham Lincoln, Volume 7* (New Brunswick, New Jersey: Rutgers University Press, 1953), 543, https://quod.lib.umich.edu/l/lincoln/lincoln7/1:1184?rgn=div1;view=fulltext.
[93] "10 Quotes from Billy Graham on the Bible," Billy Graham Library, February 10, 2022, https://billygrahamlibrary.org/blog-10-quotes-from-billy-graham-on-the Bible/#:~:text=The%20Bible%20is%20more%20modern,that%20you%20will%20obey%20it.
[94] "Understanding Stare Decisis," American Bar Association, https://www.americanbar.org/groups/public_education/publications/preview_home/understand-stare-decisis.
[95] Quoted by Morgan Housel, "Five Lessons from History," May 6, 2019, https://collabfund.com/blog/five-lessons-from-history.
[96] Eric Metaxia, *Letter to the American Church* (Washington, D.C.: Salem Books, 2022), 48.
[97] Jordan Peterson Academy, "Jordan Peterson - You Can Tell Much About a Man by How Much Truth He Tolerates – Nietzsche," YouTube, April 1, 2020, https://www.youtube.com/watch?v=uFbVjCCnrtY.
[98] George Orwell, *Animal Farm: A Fairy Story* (London: Secker and Warburg,

1945), 127.

99 "Follow the Leader," Sheep 101 Information, https://www.sheep101.info/flocking.html#:~:text=Sheep%20101%3A%20she ep%20behavior&text=Sheep%20have%20a%20strong%20instinct,follow%20 each%20other%20to%20slaughter.

100 Rick Mayer, "A John's Hopkins Study Says Ill-Founded COVID Lockdowns Did More Harm than Good," Health News Florida, February 2, 2022, https://health.wusf.usf.edu/health-news-florida/2022-02-02/a-johns-hopkins-study-says-ill-founded-lockdowns-did-little-to-limit-covid-deaths.

101 Pamela Holloway, www.HealthRecoveryMinistry.Org. Which post from this website are you citing?

102 Pamela Holloway, www.radicalresilience.health. Which post from this website are you citing?

103 Dwight D. Eisenhower, Eisenhower's Farewell Speech, cited in Ibid, Author's note. This citation is unclear. Can you be more specific about where you found it?

104 NPR Staff, "The Reason Your Feed Became an Echo Chamber—and What to Do About It," NPR, July 24, 2016, https://www.npr.org/sections/alltechconsidered/2016/07/24/486941582/the-reason-your-feed-became-an-echo-chamber-and-what-to-do-about-it.

105 Noëlle Bovon, "People Are Hard to Hate Up Close," Noëlle Bovon, December 20, 2017, https://noellebovon.com/people-are-hard-to-hate-up-close.

106 Gina Barreca, "Do We Fear Listening to the Other Side?" *Times Record News*, March 24, 2017, https://www.timesrecordnews.com/story/opinion/columnists/2017/03/24/do-we-fear-listening-other-side/99587336.

107 Blog Admin, "Challenging People's Political Views and Values Makes Them Think Even Harder and Produce Better Arguments to Defend Themselves," The London School of Economics and Political Science, September 22, 2017, https://blogs.lse.ac.uk/usappblog/2017/09/22/challenging-peoples-political-views-and-values-makes-them-think-even-harder-and-produce-better-arguments-to-defend-themselves.

108 Rod Dreher, *Live Not by Lies: A Manual for Christian Dissidents* (New York: Sentinel, 2020), 93.

109 Ibid.

110 Ibid.

111 Ibid.

[112] Ibid, 97.

Habit 8: Work Out Your Problems

[113] Martijn Schirp, "Jordan Peterson Explains the Most Useful Psychological Exercise Anyone Can Do," High Existence, January 31, 2020, https://www.highexistence.com/jordan-peterson-authenticity/.
[114] Cited in Julianne Chiaet, "The Secret to Happiness Is All in Your Head," *The Guardian*, June 22, 2016, https://www.theguardian.com/defining-moment/2016/jun/22/secret-happiness-brain-positive-attitude-train-success.
[115] Wendy Suzuki, "The Brain-Changing Benefits of Exercise," TED, November 2017, https://www.ted.com/talks/wendy_suzuki_the_brain_changing_benefits_of_exercise?language=en.
[116] Ibid.
[117] Chris Melore, "Out of Shape Nation: Half of Americans Admit They Can't Touch Their Toes Without Straining," StudyFinds, July 17, 2022, https://studyfinds.org/americans-out-of-shape-cant-touch-toes/.
[118] Ibid.
[119] Amy Horton, "Study: Americans Want to Be Fit, But Don't Put in the Work," HealthDay News, June 20, 2017, https://www.upi.com/Health_News/2017/06/20/Study-Americans-want-to-be-fit-but-dont-put-in-the-work/2821497970498/.
[120] Dr. Mark Hyman, MD, "Robert F. Kennedy Jr.: Power, Corruption, Freedom & the Chronic Disease Epidemic within America," YouTube, August 2, 2023, https://www.youtube.com/watch?v=oI9Kg2naNfs.
[121] Ibid.
[122] Mayo Clinic Staff, "Exercise: 7 Benefits of Regular Activity," Mayo Clinic, August 26, 2023, https://www.mayoclinic.org/healthy-lifestyle/fitness/in-depth/exercise/art-20048389.
[123] Ibid.
[124] Mayo Clinic Staff, "Exercise: 7 Benefits of Regular Activity," Mayo Clinic, August 26, 2023, https://www.mayoclinic.org/healthy-lifestyle/fitness/in-depth/exercise/art-20048389.
[125] Tehrene Firman, "The 50 Best 5-Minute Exercises Anyone Can Do," BestLife, May 4, 2023, https://bestlifeonline.com/five-minute-exercises.
[126] "Vitamin D," National Institutes of Health, updated September 18, 2023, https://ods.od.nih.gov/factsheets/VitaminD-HealthProfessional.

Habit 9: Be Wholehearted

[127] Crossroads Initiative.
https://www.crossroadsinitiative.com/media/articles/man-fully-alive-is-the-glory-of-god-st-irenaeus/

[128] C.S. Lewis, *The Weight of Glory* (New York: MacMillan Publishing, 1941), 87.

[129] C.S. Lewis, *The Chronicles of Narnia: The Lion, the Witch, and the Wardrobe* (London: Geophray Bles, 1950), 132.

[130] Brennan Manning, *Abba's Child: The Cry of the Heart for Intimate Belonging* (Colorado Springs: NavPress, 1994), 51.

[131] Ibid, 52.

[132] *The Gifts of Imperfection*,23.

[133] Fredrick Talbot, *Churchill on Courage*, cited from *Great Contemporaries* (Thomas Nelson Publishers 1996), Introduction.